Communication
Miracles
at Work

Effective Tools and Tips for Getting the Most From Your Work Relationships

MATTHEW GILBERT

Foreword by BJ Gallagher

CONARI PRESS
Berkeley California

Conari Press books are distributed by Publishers Group West

Cover Illustration: © Artville, Getty Inc.
Cover and Book Design: Suzanne Albertson
Author Photo: Nancy Quackenbush

LIBRARY OF CONGRESS CATALOGING-IN-PUBLICATION DATA

Gilbert, Matthew.
    Communication miracles at work : effective tools and tips for getting the most from your work relationships / Matthew Gilbert.
        p.   cm.
    Includes bibliographical references (p. 231) and index.
    ISBN 1-57324-802-9
    1. Communication in organizations. 2. Interpersonal communication. 3. Interpersonal relations. I. Title.
    HD30.3 .G527 2002
    650.1'3—dc21

                                            2001007524

Printed in Canada.

02 03 04 05   TC   10 9 8 7 6 5 4 3 2 1

Communication Miracles at Work

"Organizations are no longer built on force. They are increasingly built on trust ... this presupposes that people understand one another. Taking relationship responsibility is therefore an absolute necessity. It is a duty."

—PETER DRUCKER, Management
Challenges for the 21st Century

Foreword

Foreword by BJ Gallagher, co-author of
What Would the Buddha Do at Work
and *A Peacock in the Land of Penguins*

In real estate, the three most important things are "location, location, location." In organizational life, it's "communication, communication, communication." Communication is everything. It is the number one challenge of groups both large and small. In my twenty years of experience consulting with businesses and conducting seminars, I have yet to work with a team, department, or company that didn't have communication problems. Wherever two or more people are gathered, the chance for miscommunication will be there. The more people involved, the more complex the problems.

Matthew Gilbert understands this. The thing I like best about his book, *Communication Miracles at Work,* is that it is both informative and practical. I like books that tell me something I need to know while also teaching me new skills. I like books that don't just outline a problem but suggest solutions as well.

The other thing I especially like about Gilbert's book is his emphasis on personal responsibility. I am responsible for my communication: for picking the right words and the most appropriate medium (face to face, phone, e-mail, memo, large meeting); for knowing my audience, gauging their receptivity, and speaking "into" their listening; and for enhancing the effectiveness of any communication by selecting the appropriate time and place as often as I can. Simply stated, improving communication at work starts with me. No matter where I am in my organization's hierarchy (even if I'm at the bottom!), I can take the initiative to make my communication with others more effective.

Work is first and foremost about relationships—with bosses, coworkers, clients and customers, vendors, and others. And relationships are first and foremost about communication—listening, speaking, solving problems, resolving conflicts, negotiating deals, articulating a vision, sharing values. If you're interested in building better relationships at work, if you're looking to understand others better and to have them understand you, then this insightful, well-written book is for you. If you're independently wealthy, don't have to work, and don't care about improving your relationships with others—then this book is still for you...to give to a friend! I hope that you (or your friend) will get as much out of it as I did.

Introduction

The above two comments bluntly sum up the feelings many of us have about the possibility of our workplace lives ever becoming saner. Day in and day out, our jobs can feel like battle zones of conflict, confusion, and despair, and sometimes it's all we can do not to stand up on a chair and scream. Just think about poor Dilbert and his crazy-making coworkers. His is a made-up world, of course, but how different is it really from the place you work? We laugh about it, and that's a healthy thing to do. But in the grit of the moment, when someone isn't making sense or playing fair or is saying something that you just don't want to hear, the humor is hard to find. These interactions can happen at any time and they can take many different forms.

Reflect on your own job for a moment. Do you have permission to say what you truly mean? Are your contributions valued, or do you wonder if anyone knows you're even there? How about your boss? Is he or she easy to talk to? Does he or she make an effort to understand what you need? What if an order doesn't get filled or a report is misfiled? Are mistakes thoughtfully handled, or is there a trail of blame and guilt?

In each situation communication plays a vital role, and if that process breaks down in any way, if we aren't being heard or can't resolve a conflict or haven't been acknowledged for a job well done, then even a beloved job becomes the enemy, and Mondays become a day to dread. But if our workplace relationships are productive and harmonious, if we feel our problems are taken seriously and our humanity is valued, then we really start to love what we do, and work magically energizes us.

To be sure, communicating effectively at work is a challenge. It has as much to do with what we can't control as with what we can and depends on such things as the kind of company we work for and the values it supports; whether we are male or female; whether we are high or low on the corporate ladder; and what goes on inside of us emotionally and psychologically. All this and more influences our ability to work well with others at our jobs. Understanding these influences is one of the keys to creating better workplace relations.

It's true that new digital communication tools are revolutionizing the way we connect with others; they provide an amazing immediacy and flow when you're making contact from a distance. But they won't be much help at work when the boss is bearing down on you or a customer is screaming over the phone. These are the times when true communication skills can cut through the mess like a fine blade. What we say and how we say it—the quality and intention of our words—is still more art than science, and as the workplace reinvents itself with new models and technologies and a broadening racial and ethnic mix, this art becomes ever more valuable.

A general survey of corporate executives conducted by the American Management Association concluded that communication-related conflicts—from misunderstandings, value differences, personality clashes, broken trusts, arguments over methods, and so on—take up nearly a quarter of their time! Imagine what else this energy could have been used for. Some conflict is inevitable, of course, but how often it happens and how it is dealt with will make our jobs either hum with harmony or grind with discontent.

The heart of good communication is building strong relationships and learning what it takes to keep them healthy. The true value of a company can be measured by the quality of the connections that exist among those who work there and those they serve. How they get along, how they listen to and treat each other, how they use those relationships to learn about one another and the work they do together, will make all the difference in how each one feels at the end of the day and how willing they are to come back again the next morning.

Good communication is not about convincing another person that you have the best idea or the strongest argument or the right to the final word. It's not about hiding behind a title or double-talking around a bottom line. It's not one way, and it's not about winners and losers. It's about nurturing a spirit of teamwork, problem solving, and serving the greater good. It's about choosing the kind of person you want to be and the values you want to embrace, even in the face of circumstances that seem directly opposed to your goal. Patience and strength, wisdom and compassion, honesty and truth—are all part of communicating with integrity. Work forces us into contact with other people and challenges us to be our best.

How often have you thought to yourself something like, "If for once Mr. X seriously listened to my ideas, it would be a miracle!"? Well, miracles come in large and small packages, and whether or not something really is "an extraordinary event manifesting divine intervention in human affairs" (according to Mr. Webster), it can seem that way. And besides, what to call it is less important than the fact that a breakthrough is made or an old pattern is shaken up.

This book, then, is about how to achieve those breakthrough moments, whether they be with coworkers, the boss, a client, or inside of you. It's about the challenges of and opportunities for getting what we want while serving our employer's mission, and how communication can become a tool for achieving workplace harmony and workplace results. It's for people who want to make a difference, who are tired of playing games and are willing to take some risks. You will learn about good and bad communication, the role of gender, how to deal with specific situations, and what your own obstacles to being an effective communicator are. You will become more aware of what you are bringing to your on-the-job interactions with others and what others are bringing to you. With this new awareness, you can start making new choices and turn almost any workplace encounter into an opportunity for personal growth, professional success, and a feeling of communal well-being.

CHAPTER 1

"Thinking about corporate culture might sound somewhat 'touchy feely,' but I would argue that few characteristics are more important to a company's success."

—THE MOTLEY FOOL,
a financial website

"We must learn to live together as brothers or perish together as fools."

—MARTIN LUTHER KING. JR.

Workplace Cultures

Before exploring workplace communication or the potential for miracles, let's first talk about the workplace itself and how it has (and hasn't) changed over the years. If you watch old movies, for example, you'll notice that most companies were depicted as pretty straitlaced, with lots of earnest men in their starched white shirts and conservative ties performing their narrow but important roles with a steadfast commitment. There were specific rules, chains of command, and the general drone of commerce without much variation. It was a time when companies like Ford, IBM, and General Electric ruled the Western world, where you took what these paternal giants gave you and were happy just to be a productive cog in the economic machine.

No more.

Today, with more women in the workforce, more autonomy for employees, partnering and teamwork, flextime and job shares, and growing multicultural diversity, the workplace bears little resemblance to the one to which our fathers made a lifetime commitment. Workplaces are changing with the times, spurred also by a flood of new strategies for getting more out of less: hierarchy leveling, quality circles, theories Y and Z, "best practices," and the list goes on. The goal of these strategies has been to improve workplace performance while giving management—and employees—more of that they need.

And yet despite all that effort and adaptation and, for many workers, growing wages, job satisfaction remains surprisingly low:

- A study completed in 2000 by The Conference Board, a nonprofit membership organization for business executives, found that almost half of all workers weren't happy with their jobs.

- A recent study of 1000 workers commissioned by Headhunter.net found that 78 percent of them would take a new position if the right opportunity came along, while 48 percent were actively looking for a new job.

- The Bureau of Labor Statistics reports that American workers hold on average nine different jobs before the age of thirty-two (which isn't all that amazing if you think about how many restaurant jobs you had before the age of twenty!).

According to these and other reports, the most frequently cited reasons that we leave our jobs, or would like to, include a lack of recognition, salary issues, a weak sense of purpose or mission, few opportunities for advancement, and insufficient training. Many people surveyed also reported a drop in satisfaction with their workplace relationships, historically a key component of job enjoyment.

And yet workplace benefits have never been more generous. Companies are going out of their way to meet their employees' needs, sometimes out of a true sense of giving, sometimes as a desperate measure to keep staff, and sometimes as a response when cries for change can no longer be ignored. Many of these changes are designed to help working folks better integrate their personal lives with their professional lives. And still they don't seem to be enough.

What's going on here? From what well does such deep dissatisfaction draw?

Sure, there are legitimate problems in our workplaces, many of which will be discussed in the pages that follow. Workplace stress, much of it fueled by dysfunctional relationships and communication breakdowns, has never been higher. But maybe we're asking for too much from our jobs. Should work be all things to all people? Can it be? Are acknowledgment, a big paycheck, limitless potential, and limited hassles more than any company should be expected to give?

Wanting It All

In 1943, psychologist Abraham Maslow presented his famous "hierarchy of needs" theory. At the bottom of the pyramid are the basics: food, water, shelter. Then there is safety and security (money). Next come social needs (a sense of belonging, love), then ego needs (self-esteem, respect from others), and finally self-actualization—achieving our highest potential. It was a process he felt that all human beings are born to follow, the natural stages of human maturation. But is it a process that stops at the office door? Perhaps it's unrealistic to think that we can meet all our higher needs at our jobs. There are many who believe that our expectations have simply become too high, that our jobs were never meant to provide much more than a fair wage and a reasonably pleasant place to work.

This claim was best expressed in a provocative article entitled "The Myth of Job Happiness" in *Workforce,* a magazine for "human resource" professionals. It quoted both an author and a professor defending the notion that the problem of workplace dissatisfaction lies not with the companies but with their workers. The author, Dave Arnott (who wrote *Corporate Cults: The Insidious Lure of the All-Consuming Organization*), believes that "employees are expecting the wrong things from the workplace. They are expecting emotional satisfaction from work, not just financial satisfaction."

Professor of leisure studies Benjamin Hunnicutt goes even further, stating, "It's a myth that we can find identity, meaning, and community at work." He calls this the "Mary Tyler Moore myth," a reference to the optimistic heroine of television sitcom fame. "In reality," he says, "employees find dullards and irrational bosses" because the politics of work "is about control."

Well, he's right up to a point. But the whole purpose of what came to be called by management theorists the "human relations movement" was to counteract the task-oriented models of workplace performance with a more people-centered perspective. And while it's also true that work has taken up more and more space in our lives, what's wrong with a company with a healthy sense of community, where people working together can stretch for something larger than the next paycheck? Our jobs shouldn't supplant a healthy life outside of work where family, friends, and being in nature take precedent, but if we leave too much of ourselves at home, our performance at work can only suffer, and so too will the company that employs us.

And don't assume that companies or groups whose primary mission is to save the world have it any easier. These workplaces can be just as dysfunctional as any glass-towered corporate Goliath. Having worked with Green Party USA in the early 1990s, I can tell you that just because a group of people is committed to lofty goals of societal and planetary change doesn't mean it knows

> What's wrong with a company with a healthy sense of community, where people working together can stretch for something larger than the next paycheck?

how to work together or to get a job done. In fact, with so much passion and purpose on the line, the organization's members spent as much time figuring out how to get along as they did working on how to actually get their messages out. Ironically, though, by focusing so much energy on an inclusive process of making decisions, they *were* changing the world, one disagreement at a time.

Corporate Personality

Fortunately there are companies—more than you may think—that receive consistently high marks for employee satisfaction, have low rates of turnover, and earn impressive financial returns. They have integrated corporate values and personal values into a way of doing business that honors the need for both. The recipe for success is slightly different for each, but they all share characteristics that make them stand out in a crowd.

This is where the nitty-gritty of workplace culture comes in.

In short, workplace culture is defined by a company's mission, goals, and values and by how those things influence the working environment itself and the behaviors of those who work there. It's basically what differentiates working for one company from working for another. From the pressed-suit rigidity of Wall Street to the "anything goes" philosophy of dot.coms (at least in the early days), each company has its own spoken and unspoken rules of conduct, further influenced by societal standards and gender conditioning of what is and isn't OK.

Hospitals, for example, are in the business of preserving and saving lives, and that overarching commitment affects the urgency with which that mission is carried out. A cake factory, by comparison, will probably have an entirely different atmosphere. Yes, there may be an urgency to getting cakes in the box and out the door, but they are cakes, not people (just imagine the fringe benefits, though!).

But even companies in the same business can have very diverse dispositions. When I was working in the casino business back in the late 1970s, there was an establishment on every corner and quite a few in between, but each one was slightly different. There were the high-roller hotels, where dealers were expected to act with a certain decorum. Chatting with the customers was discouraged, and the dress and grooming codes were strictly enforced. In others, the prevailing attitude was that the fewer rules, the better. A truck-stop casino near Reno, the last chance to gamble before crossing the state line into California, was famous as a place where dealer-customer repartée was part of the show. The friendlier you were, the more likely you'd walk away at the end of the night with a pocketful of tips.

To get a better sense of your workplace culture, think of it as having a personality. Is it loose or rigid, fun or serious, caring or cold? Could it be characterized as a race car driver, a mother hen, a stuffy patriarch, an absent-minded professor? Is it more like Gordon Gecko, the character in the movie *Wall Street,* ready to eat someone's lunch at a moment's notice, or like good-guy banker Jimmy Stewart in *It's a Wonderful Life?* Is it the kind of place where honesty and respect are considered fundamental corporate values, or is it nose-to-the-grindstone, don't ask questions, punch the clock, and go home?

What does all this have to do with communication? A lot, because the more a company encourages openness, camaraderie, and teamwork on the job, the more fertile the conditions for a communication miracle to occur. In fact, the more open and human-centered the company, the more likely that a communication breakthrough will seem like an everyday part of business and not a miracle. A manager goes out of her way to ensure that an employee has what he needs to do his job. A co-worker will make it a point to be friendly to a shy new hire. The boss of the entire company asks you what should be done about the new federal regulations.

> The more a company encourages openness, camaraderie, and teamwork on the job, the more fertile the conditions for a communication miracle to occur.

And so how we communicate at our jobs—what, where, when, why, and with whom—is influenced by what is and isn't valued in our company's particular culture.

Is Your Company a "Great Place to Work"?

Believe it or not, there is an organization called Great Place to Work® Institute, which for the last several years has identified companies whose workplace cultures resonate with the kind of qualities that keep employees satisfied and loyal. They publish an annual list entitled "The 100 Best Companies to Work For," which occupies significant editorial space in each year's January edition of *Fortune* magazine.

Institute founder Robert Levering defines a "great place to work" as one where you "trust the people you work with, have pride in what you do, and enjoy the people you work with." As Levering and his associates see it, trust is measured by credibility ("Are managers approachable? Do they deliver on their promises?"), respect ("Are your contributions recognized and your ideas sought out?" "Does the company realize that you have a personal life?"), and fairness ("Is good work properly rewarded? Is everyone treated equally?"). Pride is about the job itself: Does your work have meaning? Is it helping to make the world a better place? And finally, it is measured by camaraderie: Is your workplace friendly? Do you feel like you can be yourself? If you answer yes to all these questions, you've struck it rich!

The institute's work confirms the belief that the real reason people stay in the same job is not because of an impressive benefits package or the latest technological tools, but because their work satisfies and fulfills them on a deeper level. How one feels at work and the quality of the relationships they have with others are often at the heart of their contentedness. Such an experience of what a company and its people are capable of can inspire the kind of loyalty that money just can't buy.

The TDI Story

TDIndustries is a construction and service company that has provided a variety of mechanical, electrical, plumbing, and energy services to customers in Texas and throughout the Southwest for more than fifty years. It has been a consistent high scorer in the institute's "Top-100" rankings, is employee owned—which says something about the company's commitment to those who work there—and staff loyalty is legendary. The mission statement reads, in part, that the company "focuses on our customers as the engine which drives our ability to provide outstanding careers for all of our employee owners and security for their families."

Spokesperson Jessie McCain explains that TDI's success is largely the result of "our concern for and belief in individual human beings. We believe that the individual has dignity and importance, that people are basically honest, and that each person wants to do a good job. We believe that no one has ever really found the limits of human ability. In addition, [we value] individual differences, honesty, building trusting relationships, fairness, responsible behavior, and high standards of business ethics."

This sounds very impressive, doesn't it? It's important to know, though, that TDI's accomplishments didn't happen overnight. They are the result of a long and persevering process, both a bottom-up and top-down commitment, which McCain describes as "long experience with mistakes and triumphs, and a spirit that sustains and uplifts." And a big part of their success has been their emphasis on communication.

The company has what it calls a "no-door" policy. This means that anyone can visit anyone else at any time. If the mail clerk has a bone to pick with the vice president of distribution, he or she is encouraged to do so. In fact, says McCain, "Our wonderful CEO, Jack Lowe, is disappointed if "partners" (all employees are considered partners) do not visit him. Jack leads a series of meetings every few weeks where a group of thirty or so partners are invited to have breakfast with him to discuss anything that is on their minds. The meetings are called Partner Roundtables and have been a very effective vehicle for letting Jack 'in on the grapevine' and knowing what is concerning our workers."

TDIndustries also believes in "open-book management." On one Friday each month they discuss with anyone who can attend all sales and forecast information "so everyone will know where we are from a financial standpoint."

TDI empowers its employees to resolve problems at their source. "The person closest to the problem is probably the one who knows best how to correct it!" says McCain. "We aren't a very formal or structured company, but somehow we're usually able to solve most of our problems without mediation or formal review. When you get conflicting parties together in the same room with a win-win attitude, there isn't much you can't accomplish together."

Finally, TDI has an extensive "new partner" orientation process that spans a two-year period and covers everything from the company's culture and benefits to its emphasis on quality and opportunities for growth. "Needless to say," McCain enthuses, "*communication* is the key word at TDIndustries. In fact, we've been accused of overcommunicating!"

Assessing Your Company's Culture

Now, all of this is well and good. We applaud the TDIs of the world (and you'll read about more of them in chapter 8). We love the idea of an open, honest, functional workplace where everyone is treated like a human being, where there are no real bad guys, and where sales goals are always met. But in reality, the workplace is usually a very mixed bag. You may love your co-workers but think your boss is a loser. There may be a great benefits package, but mistakes are treated harshly. There may be an open-door policy with management, but perhaps your ideas are never implemented.

So it's important to get a better handle on the culture of your workplace—its strengths and weaknesses, its written and unwritten codes of conduct—and how those things affect your comfort level and performance. Once you determine the kind of company you work for, you will start to understand how that "corporate personality" influences your interactions with others.

In general, companies tend to be characterized by certain traits, and one simple way to categorize them would be by whether they emphasize power and control or partnership and openness; competition and fear or cooperation and trust; quantity or quality; individuals or the group. The following key areas, common to all companies, are described using a series of questions. Each answer will reveal an aspect of your work culture. Some will be more important to you than others, but all of them will have an impact on the person you are at work and the person you want to be.

> It's important to get a better handle on the culture of your workplace—its strengths and weaknesses, its written and unwritten codes of conduct—and how those things affect your comfort level and performance.

Mission and Purpose

Does the company have a clear vision of what it is and where it's going, and does it communicate this to employees? Does this vision guide specific actions and behavior, or is it mostly just empty words? Do you know the part you play in realizing that vision? To what values does the company hold fast?

Leadership and Management

Do you trust and respect the people "in charge"? Do they walk their talk? Do they inspire you to be loyal and to work hard? Are there clear lines of responsibility—does the buck stop somewhere? Do they treat you with respect, like a real human being? Is abuse dealt with quickly and fairly? Who holds the real power in the company?

Information and Communication

Do you learn everything you need to know about the company and your particular job through normal channels, or do you have to rely on unofficial channels like the office "grapevine"? Do people tend to say one thing and do another? Is information generally out in the open, or does the atmosphere feel secretive and covert? When you were first hired, was anything said that you later found out wasn't true or completely accurate? Maybe there's too much information of the wrong kind. Mike, a systems administrator for a regional utility company, laments that "having to sift through hundreds of e-mails every week takes a toll on getting my work done."

Decision-Making and Problem Solving

Are you comfortable asking for help or bringing problems to a boss or coworker? Do they ask for, and then listen seriously to, your suggestions? How are mistakes and complaints generally handled? Are they dealt with thoughtfully, without blame, and with input from many, or with anger and criticism and "you're on your own" solutions? Do you feel you have a role in decision making, or are you often the last to know? Is there a spirit of teamwork in the face of a challenge? Is the dominant workplace attitude win-win or win-lose?

Feedback and Recognition

How does your company define success? As meeting or exceeding goals? As taking risks? As low turnover? As happy workers? How do people get ahead in your company? What kinds of behavior are rewarded? What skills, characteristics, and accomplishments does your workplace value? Do you feel you get enough recognition for your contributions? When and how do you get it? How are feedback and criticism delivered—in a one-way communication or with a more constructive give-and-take? Are managers receptive to evaluations of their own performances?

Encouraging Diversity

Does your workplace have a healthy mix of ethnic diversity? Does the blend of people in management and leadership positions reflect the ethnic and gender diversity of the overall company? Do people from different cultures—including the United States—mingle easily with one another, or do they tend to stay in their own groups? Does your company actively support training in cultural sensitivity and diversity awareness? Is this training ongoing or one time or sporadic?

Formality and Socializing

How do people greet one another? Is it Mr. X and Mrs. Y or first names, regardless of position? How do people dress? Is there a high level of openness and disclosure? Are there cliques? If so, can people comfortably socialize between different ones? Do people tend to keep their personal life separate from their work life? Is everyone "in this thing together," or is it every man and woman for themselves? Is intra-office camaraderie encouraged or discouraged? Is this encouragement or discouragement subtle or more up-front?

The Workspace

Do you work in an open or closed work area? Is the space designed so that people can mingle easily with others? Do you notice personalized items such as photos, pictures, plants, or knickknacks? Is eating allowed in your workspace? Can you make personal calls on your breaks? Do people stay where they are to take breaks, or do they go someplace else, such as off-grounds or to the coffee room?

The Intangibles

What is your gut feeling about where you work? Do you feel comfortable in your bones when you're there, or does something always feel a little off? How easy is it to be yourself? Would you recommend your company to others? Why? Why not?

Beyond the Status Quo

The buzzwords these days are *partnership* and *cooperation,* because it has finally sunk in that to do a job well we often need to work *with* others, not against them. The most successful and enjoyable companies are those that place a high value on working together and building strong relationships, which makes good communication vital. In fact, you can't have one without the other.

> The buzzwords these days are *partnership* and *cooperation*, because it has finally sunk in that to do a job well we often need to work *with* others, not against them.

In *From Chaos to Confidence: Survival Strategies for the New Workplace,* Susan Campbell talks about how organizations are changing to survive and thrive in the twenty-first century.

> New organizational forms are emerging that put each person in a feedback loop where her ideas, thoughts, and feelings can be more quickly and readily heard, learned from, and updated. This means changing the unwritten rules in our organizations and changing how workers perceive themselves. It could mean, for example, inviting people from various fields in the organization to sit down together in a meeting that use to be attended only by officers. It

will undoubtedly mean that leaders need to get comfortable sharing decision making.

Communication miracles happen when there is an intention to go beyond the status quo, beyond the way things have always been done. It happens in companies that are committed to bringing out your best, to providing models and incentives for making real connections with colleagues. This doesn't guarantee that every interaction will be a pleasant one, or that there won't be problems too difficult to get through without a little pain. But workplace culture can have a powerful influence. Recognizing the subtleties of that influence on our behavior and on that of our coworkers is an important first step toward taking more control, making new choices, and experiencing the kind of communication breakthroughs that satisfy at a deep enough level to count.

CHAPTER 2

"Along this tree, from root to crown, ideas flow up, and vetoes down."

—ANONYMOUS EXECUTIVE

"For every minute you remain angry, you give up sixty seconds of peace of mind."

—RALPH WALDO EMERSON

Why Am I So Mad?

The ability—indeed the willingness—to communicate honestly, confidently, and compassionately at work will be nearly impossible if something about your job is bothering you, which often means there's anger or even fear. If either or both of these feelings have become your steady workplace companions, then resentment or insecurity won't be far behind, and almost anything you say or do will be tainted by them. Your spirits will sink, and your relationships will suffer.

But don't feel guilty if your job has you grinding your teeth at night; glitch-free workplaces are rare. Even the healthiest companies, the "best place to work" utopias described in chapter 1, aren't immune from the unpredictable forces that beget dissatisfaction. When you consider all the different ways that wires can cross—what with dysfunctional company cultures and the pressures of performance and each person's personal style and needs—it's a wonder that we can get anything done at all! "There's a lot of devious behavior out there," said one disillusioned consultant. "People say one thing and do another. They have a public face and a behind-the-scenes face. When it comes down to communication, what is said and how it's said, it's all about politics. I don't think many people *want* to support their company—they're angry!"

Indeed, scratch the surface of many corporate veneers and you'll likely find plenty of simmering turmoil. The Workplace Violence Research Institute has estimated that on-the-job violence costs employers more than $36 billion annually, an *850 percent increase* during the past five years. A recent Gallup poll found that 25 percent of those surveyed about workplace issues considered themselves "somewhat angry" while on the job. In another study, 42 percent of those surveyed reported experiencing verbal abuse on the job, 29 percent had screamed at a coworker, and 23 percent had cried over workplace frustrations. One magazine publisher called it "desk rage." And while surveys are hardly reliable barometers of ultimate truth, the results indicate that our places of work can be real emotional battlegrounds.

What these reports didn't explain, though, is why these people were angry or what they meant by "verbal abuse." What prompted someone to actually scream at a coworker? These are powerful reactions, and yet I can recall at least one example of each incident mentioned above at every place I have worked, and that's quite a few places. Most of those outbursts had little to do with the actual work being done and a lot to do with unresolved frustrations with coworkers or management or the customers being served. In other words—people problems.

The "tipping point" in many of these instances is stress—when our emotional cool finally overheats from a steady accumulation of tensions. Some people simply run out of patience with a bullying boss whose sport of choice is to badger and berate. Others bring difficult home situations to work and act out their issues with the first person to get in their way. Perhaps an unreasonable workload with no light at the end of the tunnel finally pushes someone over the edge. We are only human, after all, trying to make the best of difficult situations, and sometimes the dam simply breaks.

"Hospitals are terrible places lately," Marie explained when I asked about her work. She's been a nurse for years and loves what she does—especially the relationships she has with her patients—but has seen a lot of changes lately that are making it more difficult to experience the satisfaction she felt when she first started. She's angry about what's happening but doesn't know what to do. "They talk a lot about patient care as their main goal, but money is the bottom line. Many of them are restructuring and re-engineering to get rid of more people. Most of the time it's in the clinical areas—nursing, respiratory therapists—so everyone's miserable because you can't accomplish the real bottom line—good patient care—while you're overworking the staff."

Marie's frustration is palpable, but her situation is typical of the kind of patience-testing environments that many of us deal with every day. Some of the problems are preventable, some of them aren't. Some you have control over, and some you don't. As we'll discuss later, learning to

> The sources of work-place anger are many, and their impacts are often subtle.

discern which is which is part of the road to resolution. For now, let's take a look at the different ways that work makes it tough for us to be our best and to connect with others in a healthy and life-affirming way.

Who—or What—Is Getting Under My Skin?

The sources of workplace anger are many, and their impacts are often subtle. Most of the time we try to ignore them and go about our business, hoping that maybe they'll go away and tomorrow will be different. But they don't go away. The discontent builds, our job performance suffers, and we start carrying the weight of it all home with us. It's an insidious process, sabotaging our equilibrium and making us feel rebellious and unsafe. It's been said that there are two kinds of employees: those who quit and leave, and those who quit and stay.

Take a moment and consider the following list of stress points. Some are specific, while others are more general. Some may be affecting the way you behave and feel about yourself at work.

- You aren't taken seriously or listened to or respected.
- Your efforts go unrecognized.

- You aren't paid what you're worth relative to what others are making.

- Others seem to get preferential treatment.

- In this company, it's not how well you do but who you know.

- You're generally afraid to speak up about a problem or a situation.

- You don't feel like you're part of a team working toward a common goal.

- There's too much gossiping and secrecy.

- The company or a coworker has betrayed you in some way.

- People don't keep their word; you're promised one thing but given another.

- You haven't met your own or another's expectations.

- Someone has openly criticized you; your credibility has been questioned.

- You lost a key assignment.

- You get left out of the loop too often.

- The demands of your job have become unreasonable; the workload has become too much.

- You don't feel you have enough control over what you do.

- The work you do has become boring or dissatisfying; it is no longer meaningful.

- There are no opportunities for advancement.

- Your boss is a jerk.

Looking closely at the list, do you identify any items that apply to you? If so, how do they make you feel? Angry, scared, frustrated, depressed? Can you connect the emotions you're experiencing with specific situations at work? Which ones and with which people? Are the stress points always the same—that Friday afternoon report or tyrannical Mr. Jones—or are they more widespread?

Now, some of this stuff happens to all of us at one place or another, and it's not unusual for them to pass with time or with new people or as the result of a small adjustment in attitude. But if our good intentions continue to be thwarted by uncaring managers or clueless coworkers or by our own inability to take a right action, we convince ourselves— rightly or wrongly—that a solution is impossible, and that realization hits us in our emotional center. Anger is the most common response, but so are confusion or fear or despair. Different people react in different ways.

The angry ones are the easiest to notice. They're cynical and edgy. They'll take any opportunity to talk the company or a coworker down, but they aren't likely to seek a real solution to their problem. For different reasons they are invested in their discontent. Beware of these folks around the water cooler; they're usually looking for sympathizers and recruits while strategizing their revenge. Others act out their anger more subtly, keeping their feelings to themselves while quietly getting even. The punishments in either case can take many forms, from longer lunch breaks and cutting corners on performance to lying, stealing, withholding information, and even selling secrets to the competition. Anything is justified if we truly feel mistreated!

Other people simply lose hope, letting the system or the process grind them down. They may withdraw into disillusionment or go deeper into insecurity and self-doubt as they internalize the burden of defeat. "There's nothing I can do," they will say. "Things will never change." Their own feelings of low self-worth are reinforced. They cope. Their work becomes an energy-sapping drudgery. There can be physical symptoms as well: ulcers, fatigue, weight problems, insomnia, depression.

Neither type described above takes much—if any—responsibility for their actions or their situation. The angry ones will blame others, convinced that the mess they're in is someone else's fault. Those who have lost hope may blame another for their problems, but they also blame themselves. No matter how the blame game is played, it will prevent the possibility for a lasting solution to be found.

A small minority will face their torment head-on, methodically and intuitively deciding what steps they need to take and then putting those decisions into action. Communicating directly with a colleague or a manager is often part of the plan. Since sensitive issues may be involved, good preparation is vital: deciding what to say, how to say it, and what to do if you don't get the results you want. This strategy won't guarantee success, but these courageous few are willing to take the risk because they're committed to uncovering the truth, to building good relations, and—pardon the cliché—to being the best that they can be. It's important to note that they make this kind of effort as much for themselves as for the company. This is the most honorable way to respond to such challenges, but also the most difficult, because it requires us to go beyond our normal limits.

The Triumph of Anger and Fear

Those who succumb to anger or defeat have chosen a road well traveled. The powers that be are too strong, they will say, while their own willingness to step forward is too weak. Many studies have shown that the biggest reason people don't talk honestly about problems at work is fear of repercussion. And since our jobs play such a major role in our lives, this disincentive, however real or implied, is a strong one.

Richard Barrett, a former World Bank executive and now a business consultant and author (*Liberating the Corporate Soul,* among others), said in a *Personnel Journal* interview, "Fear is one of the great destroyers of community, particularly community in the workplace.... [It doesn't support] an atmosphere conducive to liberating the intuition and creativity that can come from a deeper level."

But let's be realistic: Speaking up about something that's troubling you can be an iffy proposition at work, especially when honesty isn't encouraged. Companies can be frightfully oppressive places, with unspoken rules of what is and isn't accepted. A lot of executives say they want creative people, but individual personalities are usually molded to fit the culture. The pressure to be a team player keeps the lid on a lot of issues. Look at how many years it took for tobacco industry insiders to step forward and expose the criminal violations that were an everyday part of doing business. The movie *The Insider,* about the life of a key witness in the prosecution of Big Tobacco, made clear that taking such courageous action is a high-stakes decision. Whistle-blowing is inarguably a heroic and selfless act, but it takes a tremendous amount of principle and perseverance.

Most of the challenges we deal with at work are hardly of such headline-making drama, but they are real enough and affect us in many ways. The majority of us want to do our best on the job, but to feel powerless in the face of problems that are making our work lives miserable is debilitating. It means we can't move forward. It means we've lost meaningful contact with our colleagues and lost trust in the company for which we work.

> Speaking up about something that's troubling you can be an iffy proposition at work, especially when honesty isn't encouraged.

We take what we do very personally, and so there will be hurt feelings and bruised egos and mounting feelings of isolation. The workplace quickly devolves into a "me versus them" battleground.

In times like these it doesn't help that most of us have to deal with a hierarchical system of relationships and decision making. For example, unless you're the owner or the CEO, you have a boss, and by this definition most of us have one. Usually this system works well enough; the buck has to stop somewhere. But what happens if your boss is taking advantage of his position? When discussing anger and fear at work, issues of power—who has it, how they use it, how one feels when they are under it—inevitably come up, and so if someone with more power than you isn't treating you with respect, it puts you in a bind.

In some cases the anger we feel has its roots in our childhoods. Most of the time we were told what to do "for our own good" or because Mom and Dad "know better," and whether we liked it or not we obeyed—or else. Presumably only later did the wisdom of their actions sink in. Still, there are few among us who haven't taken at least some of those frustrations into adulthood, however repressed or subconscious. At work, that childhood dynamic and those same emotions are never far away. If someone is misusing power, if they aren't playing fair, those emotions can be triggered, and suddenly we're in a familiar predicament. If we can't get resolution, if we're unable or unwilling to communicate our feelings or to process our anger or fear safely, we'll usually displace our frustrations in other, less healthy ways. And, ironically, that can mean we abuse what little power we do have.

Rosabeth Moss Kanter, in her ground-breaking 1977 book *Men and Women of the Corporation,* stated that "wronged" employees often redirect their frustrations toward those with less power than they or hold on to the power they have more fiercely and rigidly, becoming tyrannical and controlling themselves. Let's call it the "little fiefdom" effect. Unfortunately, she says, such coping mechanisms tend to reinforce the "lesser-than" position that one may be trying to avoid. In other words, acting out feelings of powerlessness in this way has the potential of producing the very characteristics commonly associated with lower status: bossiness, strictness, pettiness, defensiveness, and so on. In short, it can become a vicious circle. Honest communication becomes impossible, and relationships continue to break down. This can happen at any point on the organizational chart, from the lowest line worker (he insults the janitor) to corporate vice presidents (they have lots of people they can pick on).

The Price of Silence

As you can see, there are many varieties of workplace frustration, and a variety of ways to respond. The most common— getting even, giving up, getting out—avoid direct confrontation while offering little more than temporary relief, because the negativity is never resolved. It lingers, continuing to sabotage workplace peace of mind. When we choose not to deal with a situation or an individual that is causing us grief, or when we give up too easily, we sell ourselves short while letting the company or the injuring party off the hook. We also lose a chance for mutual growth, because we don't give others an opportunity to step forward and act from a more conscious place. In the end it may not make a difference no matter what you try, but not trying at all is the greater sin.

When we don't act on what we know to be true, or at least raise issues that need to be explored, nothing will ever change. That's the price we pay for our silence. "Quality is impossible when people are afraid to tell the truth," management guru W. Edwards Deming once said. And spiritual quality also suffers. When we don't take the chance to break new ground, to surprise ourselves with what we're capable of, we forget that transformation can occur at almost any time in almost any situation. It's a belief that can sustain you, no matter how rough the seas. It doesn't mean that every situation will change, or that every person who is part of a problem will miraculously see the light. But without faith in the possibility, we stop trying and thus help to perpetuate the spiral of dysfunction.

Of course mere belief isn't enough. You've got to take action, and that usually involves some risk, personal as well as professional. Fortunately, such initiative is like a muscle that needs to be exercised. The more we use it, the stronger it will get, and the more likely you'll start seeing results. And when you stop playing the game of silence or denial, when you decide to take an honest look at what is happening and why, you start playing a different game. Most people won't want to play that game—at least at first—because it means that real truths will be exposed,

> When we don't act on what we know to be true, or at least raise issues that need to be explored, nothing will ever change.

which is pretty scary for those who want to keep them hidden. But when you go ahead and play anyway, you're giving permission to others to play the same game, and suddenly a door opens to another way of being, another way of "doing business." Someone has to take the first step. Why not you?

Karen worked in a small specialty retail shop owned by an elder statesman, Richard Castle, in a small Northwest town. Richard, a retired military man, was a benevolent patriarch with a vexing tendency to intimidate. On some days he was a tyrant; on others he was a model of generosity. Karen never knew what to expect, but over time the two had developed an amiable enough working relationship.

"One time he was really demeaning," she recalls, "and it just cut right through me. He was trying to find fault when there wasn't any, and I was getting pretty upset. I felt like he wasn't respecting me, even though I had proven myself many times before." When she couldn't take it anymore, Karen stopped what she was doing and turned to him. She knew that the good Mr. Castle was there somewhere, and she decided to appeal to that person. She took a big breath.

"Mr. Castle," she started carefully, not entirely sure if she was doing the right thing, "I know you wouldn't speak to me like this if you knew how it felt to me."

The older man stopped what he was doing and looked back at her. His face, which had been stonily set in "business-as-usual" mode, suddenly softened. He got up from his desk, walked over to Karen, and hugged her. It was a special moment, and needless to say, the energy shifted immediately and harmony was restored.

Karen's may have been a special case, since it was just the two of them and they had a history together. But he was still her boss, the verbal abuse had been real, and Karen had been very uncomfortable. She took a big emotional risk, because the pain she felt was stronger than the part of her that was willing to just accept what was happening. Still, it's tough to communicate successfully when the mind is filled with negative thoughts and the first words waiting to rush out have no purpose other than to protect or attack or simply to release the tension.

The workplace has few outlets for dealing with such stresses. Unless you work for a very large—or very progressive—company, you won't have the luxury of a staff psychologist dedicated to the emotional health of the people who work there. Some companies do offer stress-management courses, but if the source of the problem persists, if no changes are made in the workplace itself or in how the business is run, then what is learned in those classes can be lost, and you're basically left to fend for yourself.

Returning to Center

However justified our feelings, it's vitally important to not let them cloud our capacity to see and think clearly when things at work overwhelm us. It's certainly OK—and usually necessary—to burn off our frustrations safely and appropriately, anything from a long walk to yelling in a closet to pounding our fists on a pillow. But when our feelings get the upper hand, when we make someone else the enemy, we've completely rearranged the rules of that relationship, at least temporarily. At this point we can no longer work constructively toward resolution, and in fact may have made things worse by escalating the problem into something much larger than it was. Emotions tend to feed off one another, and when they are painful, a blown lid isn't far behind. The challenge is attuning oneself to signs of emotional stress, and then doing what is necessary to return to inner balance. Addressing those stress points—whether from a

> The challenge is attuning oneself to signs of emotional stress, and then doing what is necessary to return to inner balance.

specific incidence or a build-up of frustration—begins the process of healing and transformation.

1. *Communicate with yourself.* One of the first steps to communication integrity and conscious relationship building at work is being honest about what you're experiencing. Most feelings fall into one of four categories: mad, sad, glad, or scared. There are variations, of course, and perhaps a few judgment calls—frustration might be either anger or fear—but the theory of four essential emotions usually holds true. It can get tricky, though, because the first emotion we feel may not be the one that is driving our reaction. For example, an angry outburst at a coworker who smugly reports on a "wonderful lunch" with the boss may be masking jealousy or job insecurities, which have more to do with fear. In fact, anger often acts like a big brother to protect more vulnerable feelings. Knowing which emotion is really in charge will help you respond more appropriately when a difficult encounter takes place and will bring you closer to what you need to start feeling whole again.

2. *Attend to the pain.* Whenever strong emotions have been stirred up, either from a recent single incident or a situation that has been building up over time, you need to take care of those feelings before moving on to other steps. Unresolved conflicts within you will make it that much more difficult to resolve them with

a coworker, a boss, or a client, even though any or all of them may be the source of your discontent. Set aside some quiet time so you can focus on those feelings. Let them roam free for a while; the more you resist them, the stronger they'll become. Connect with your inner voice and wisdom. Know that whatever happened or is happening is not a reflection on your value as a person. There are reasons for what occurred, there may be valuable lessons to learn, and you'll probably look back on it all as a gift (though maybe you'd like nicer packaging on the next one...).

3. *Detach from the drama.* Try to see yourself as a player on a stage and your emotion as one of the props. This detachment will put you "in the situation but not of it." You are there, but the drama isn't wrapped around you like a straitjacket. Now you've made a space—however small—to think more clearly, to allow a deeper, more clear-headed part of you to step forward with its wisdom. This is harder to do in the heat of an uncomfortable moment, of course, but with practice—paying particular attention to your breath and to relaxing your body—it will become easier and easier.

4. *Observe what happened.* With your emotions on hold, you can step back and see more clearly just what set you off. Who did what? How did it make you feel? Is this the first time or is it a pattern? In *Beyond*

Blame, Jeffrey Kottler writes that emotional upset at work is generally triggered by one of four things: not being appreciated, being undermined, feeling that someone is trying to control you, or fearing you'll end up on the wrong end of a win-lose situation. And remember that the problem may be the company itself. As you read in chapter 1, there are many things that companies do—and don't do—to sabotage the trust and loyalty of their employees.

5. *Determine what's at stake.* Decide on the gravity of the situation. Is it merely a battle of egos or something more serious, a situation that challenges your credibility or threatens your job? This practice will help you identify the fights worth fighting and also which situations are more amenable to problem-solving than others. If your beef is with a long-time corporate policy, for example, then a lot is at stake, but you'll probably have an uphill struggle. It also helps to know what is controllable and what isn't before attempting to confront a situation. It's one thing to complain when a supervisor isn't giving you clear feedback on performance, and quite another to argue that your performance would improve if the company relocated to Bermuda. This puts me in mind of the Serenity Prayer from Alcoholics Anonymous: "God, please grant me the serenity to accept those things I cannot change, the courage to change those things I can, and

the wisdom to know the difference."

6. *Isolate your part and take responsibility.* Ask yourself, "What am I bringing to this situation? How am I part of the problem? What could I have done to help prevent it?" Figuring out what is yours and what is "theirs" is a key to

> Ask yourself, "What am I bringing to this situation? How am I part of the problem? What could I have done to help prevent it?"

resolution, because while your feelings are legitimate, the problem is not always another person's fault, and sometimes it's purely situational. Is a childhood pattern being triggered? Is something else bothering you—perhaps a personal issue—that you've displaced on to the workplace? Has someone been aggravated by something about you? Is it simply a bad day for no discernible reason other than that life can be a drag? Don't forget how complicated things can get at work with corporate cultures, project pressures, personal idiosyncrasies, and even planetary alignments all colliding on any given day.

7. *Decide what to do next.* Now that you've taken care of your feelings and gathered all the information you can about what happened (or is happening) and why, it's time to make some decisions. What's the worst that

could happen if you try to resolve the problem? What if you don't? If you can let this one go—it's not a fight worth fighting—then do what you must to make peace with it and move on. Forgiveness and compassion may be part of this process; they are powerful tools for healing. If you decide that the situation requires stronger action, then make a plan. Visualize and affirm what you need to do and how. Whom do you need to talk to, what do you need to say? Don't be afraid to ask for support from family, friends, or coworkers. Devise a back-up plan if things don't go as you hope. It may be as simple as knowing you did your best and going forward with more confidence or actually leaving for greener pastures.

The Power of Action

A willingness to confront our workplace frustrations is a huge first step toward improving our relationships and our communications with others. As you will see in the following chapters, there will always be issues that threaten harmony between you and the people you work with, even in the best of companies. Some will be one-time events, others the result of long-simmering difficulties. Some will be surprisingly easy to deal with, others more of a challenge. Either way you won't know unless you try, and it's just not worth it to carry such burdens when there are tangible things that you can do. Where there is conflict and pain, there is also opportunity for learning and growth. The choice to act is yours.

CHAPTER 3

"Communication is a continual balancing act, juggling the conflicting needs for intimacy and independence."

—DEBORAH TANNEN

"In our civilization, men are afraid that they will not be men enough and women are afraid that they might be considered only women."

—THEODORE REIK,
Freud protégé, professor
of psychoanalysis at
Vienna University

The Gender Factor

Men and women have their own ways of dealing with the challenges of the workplace, and when those ways conflict, workplace harmony is at risk. These differences can be seen in management styles, leadership skills, approaches to decision making and goal setting: almost any situation that requires a coming together of hearts and minds toward a common purpose. We need look no further than our own personal relationships, especially those with our significant others, to see how complicated it can get when a man and a woman try to work something out together.

In some ways, of course, it's easier at the office, because the complexities that come with relationship intimacy don't usually exist—the person at the other desk probably won't be lying next to you when you flick off the light at night. But sometimes there's no less of an emotional attachment to outcomes. This attachment can trigger control issues galore, as everyone tries to do what he or she thinks is best for the company, and for themselves, while remaining unconscious of how their behavior may be hindering the

> Men shouldn't be more like women or women more like men in the workplace; we should all be seeking a balance of our inner masculine and feminine energies.

process. Failure to recognize and overcome the unique influence of gender relations on that process can create more problems than the most ruthless competitor, including stress, hard feelings, mistrust, and revenge, not to mention lost time and missed opportunities. These kinds of experiences will break, not make, your day.

Before I get into too much trouble, though, it's important to clarify that "male and female" don't mean the same thing as "masculine and feminine." The first two are anatomical, the latter two something else entirely. It's in that second set of words that many problems of—and solutions to—gender communication can be found. Indeed, what's becoming clear is not that men should be more like women or women more like men in the workplace, but that we should all be seeking a balance of our inner masculine and feminine energies, since therein lies the key to reaching our relationship-building goals at work. And when you begin to see how gender-influenced qualities have shaped the inner realities of those with whom you work, communication miracles won't be far behind.

Where It Started, Where It's Going

As most of you know, it all starts in childhood. No sooner are we out of the womb and on our wobbly feet than our moms and dads show up with dolls and miniature cookware for little Mary and toy guns and a baseball bat for little John. The girls immediately start developing their nesting and relational skills, while the boys practice defense of hearth and home while expressing their natural aggressions. And while this stereotype is starting to change as parents' awareness of holistic alternatives grows, most us grew up in such environments and can share similar recollections. Besides, God did make men and women differently and, at least in the original plan, for some pretty good reasons.

During these formative years, each gender continues to be shaped by traditional expectations of what men and women should be and, presumably, most naturally want to be. They are rewarded for different behaviors and taught to value different things. Men, of course, grow up in a much more competitive environment, where individual effort and the skills of conquest make the Top-10 lists. Bigger is better and might makes right in a black-and-white world of good and bad. At the same time, they learn that it's best to hide their feelings, to not show weakness or vulnerability. They become strangers to their own emotions.

Women, by comparison, aren't expected to be the warriors. They win points instead for being polite and helpful and good listeners. They are part of the support team, gentle problem solvers, a safe harbor from the brutality of the get-ahead world. Men hunt and fight; women gather and nest.

And I suppose it worked for a while—at least on the surface—as long as no one asked questions and we accepted our "predestined" roles. But as the world became more complicated, as we became more self-aware and began to explore more deeply what aided our inner harmony and what conspired against it, we pressed against the limitations imposed on our gender and sought new expressions for our evolving selves. Women, for example, began learning how to be more assertive, while men tried different recipes for quiche. The flexing of these new muscles has taken place as much in our work lives as it has everywhere else, propelled by fundamental changes in the makeup of Corporate America.

According to a Hudson Institute report called Workplace 2000, for example, the U.S. workplace has morphed from a predominantly white-male environment (80 percent) into one where women and people from other cultures now represent the majority. New models of integration are thus struggling to be birthed. There are no modern precedents for such a thing, and it shows in the day-to-day conflicts that often emerge from the inability of men and women and people from different cultures to respect one another's strengths and find constructive ways to communicate. These challenges are further complicated by the reality that white males—the natural benefactors of a process that rewards Type-A behavior with the highest positions—still hold much of the power in the American business world and are inclined to preserve the existing system. Not surprisingly, acting like men, or at least acting out their own aggressive potential, has became the norm for women with any ambition, and they have reinforced that management model while moving smartly up the organizational ladder.

A series of studies led by Northwestern University professor of psychology Alice Eagley ("Stereotypes as Dynamic Constructs: Women and Men of the Past, Present, and Future," 1999) confirmed that women in the workplace are increasingly perceived as becoming more competitive and individualistic (the traditional male stereotype), and that those perceptions are being backed up by research. In her column "Grizzled Young Veteran" (June 2001, eCompany.com), Penelope Trunk (a nom de plume) admitted the benefits of playing that game when she shared a few observations from her new job at a technology firm.

The consensus builder in the office, she says, is "a feather-unruffling, feelings-soothing Dartmouth MBA/Yale undergrad. Even though she's ten years older than I am and has more degrees than I do, we are equals. We are equals because I rise to confrontation while she shrinks from it. Men have given me more promotions than they have her because I have spoken up in meetings throughout my career, weighed in on heated discussions."

"The entire senior management team is made up of men," she writes, "and almost all of their direct reports are women." Her boss explains to her, "You need to understand that the top executives here are all alpha males. We fight until we get our way."

But that reality is changing, too, and it's changing in large part because this same massive influx of feminine energies is pulling—and sometimes pushing—the masculine extremes back toward the middle. Perhaps most remarkable are the findings of new studies showing that women managers outperform their male counterparts in a majority of workplace categories (*Business Week,* 20 November, 2000), and doing it their way:

- Hagberg Consulting Group in Foster City, California, carried out performance evaluations of senior managers across a wide range of industries and companies and found that women executives outranked men in forty-two of fifty-two skills measured.

- When Personnel Decisions International in Minneapolis surveyed nearly 60,000 managers, the results showed that women ranked higher than men in twenty of twenty-three areas.

- A more rigorous follow-up study designed to eliminate certain biases that some researchers felt discredited the above results found that women performed better than men in eleven of twenty-two management skills analyzed, still a surprising result for many.

In fact, it's becoming evident that the most valuable skills one can have in twenty-first-century business are those that women have historically possessed, those having to do with people and process and relationship and connection. "What's interesting is that the kinds of companies we admire today are also those that depend increasingly on female attributes," said Janice Gjertsen of Digital City New York in an article entitled, "Women and Men, Work and Power" (*Fast Company,* February 1998). "It's all about getting close to customers, striking up joint ventures, partnering with suppliers. The new CEO is a Seeder, Feeder, and Weeder—and those are women's roles."

What does all this have to do with communication? As women achieve greater parity at work, as they become more respected for the unique skills and talents they bring to their jobs, they begin to influence the communication norms at the companies for which they work. This is not just true for those in higher-level positions but in all areas of an organization where women and men work together. The very fact that women are the equals of men at work strongly suggests that their communication styles—how they interact with others, the priorities they set when building relationships—

> The most valuable skills one can have in twenty-first-century business are those that women have historically possessed, those having to do with people and process and relationship and connection.

will have to be reckoned with. "Men and women seem to be doing roughly equally effective jobs," concluded Robert Kabacoff, vice president of MRG, which conducted the follow-up study mentioned above, "but they approach their jobs differently." A closer look at those differing characteristics offers tremendous insights into where communication problems come from and where solutions may lie.

Who We Are at Work

Examining how men and women communicate differently in the workplace is a process ripe for stereotyping, but certain patterns do come up time and time again. What follows are some general observations, but I present them as feminine and masculine rather than as female and male tendencies, because they don't apply to everyone, at least not in the same way, and certainly not all the time. You'll know women at work who show some and maybe even most of the masculine patterns of expression, and men who are comfortable with a more feminine style of relating. A healthy balance is the key, for different situations require different skills and sensitivities. The important thing here is to familiarize yourself with the various characteristics, learn which ones best describe you, and then start watching for them where you work.

Those with Feminine Communication and Interaction Styles

- are more process oriented; more patient; more likely to see "shades of gray"
- are more collaborative; focused on team building and partnering
- are less turf conscious; more "win-win"
- are less concerned with personal glory
- emphasize people skills over business skills
- are good listeners, facilitators, and coaches
- think healthy relationships are more important than who's in charge
- are more nurturing and open; the downside is the "disease to please"
- like to "dialogue"; are willing to show sensitivity and emotions
- use talking as a way to exchange information, form a bond, and offer support
- think "emotional support" is important to any problem-solving process
- have a tendency to apologize more, both to acknowledge a mistake and as an expression of concern or sympathy

- are more reticent, less likely to speak up, more likely to give up their turn

- won't fight back when patronized, ignored, or disrespected; are inclined to deny their power

- are less willing to "take the lead" or take risks; would rather "take care of" or stand aside

Those with Masculine Communication and Interaction Styles

- are more comfortable in hierarchical, "command and control," formal and centralized systems of organization where "pecking orders" are clear

- are better at networking and building alliances (the "Survivor" strategy)

- are more direct and goal-oriented; have a "cut-to-the-chase" style; want solutions *now*

- are competitive, assertive; will interrupt, "take up space"

- are comfortable with statistics and facts; are linear in their decision making; value objectivity

- are action-oriented, driven, Type A, inflexible, ambitious

- are confrontational, outspoken, critical; think that "conversation is a contest" and conflict is natural

- have an aggressive give-and-take style of problem solving and testing solutions
- feel the need to prove themselves; look at tasks as challenges to overcome
- are private, individual, independent, heroic; are risk-takers; will make the "tough call"
- are more oriented toward power, toward making pressure decisions
- are afraid to show weakness or ask questions; have a "grin (or grim) and bear it" attitude
- have identities and egos closely tied to work; are more fearful; have more at stake

How and Where Conflicts Arise

As you can see from the two lists above, there are plenty of opportunities for these gender styles to collide, most often when decisions are made, when instructions are given, or when a problem needs to be resolved. Sometimes conflicts arise during something as simple as deciding how to arrange a room for a meeting: women (read: feminine style) will be more likely to encourage a circular format to maximize face-to-face contact, while men will almost always set chairs up in rows, facing in one direction. Other situations can of course be much more complicated, especially when the stakes are higher or the numbers of people involved bigger.

Sometimes the roots of a conflict are clearly emotional and/or the product of cultural conditioning, such as a man's sensitivity to "hysterical women" or a woman's intolerance of "patronizing Neanderthals." When such triggers are sprinkled into the stew of workplace demands, the pot can easily boil over as the object of frustration transforms from colleague/human being into a symbol of victimhood or oppression, however unwarranted this projection may be. In another example, where a man might be seen as forceful, assertive, and commanding, a woman may be considered pushy, aggressive, and demanding. Women who aspire to leadership positions risk being labeled as controlling, whereas men can get away with such pursuits because that is what we expect of them.

I don't mean to single out men as the biggest perpetrators of workplace dysfunction, but because they have been in this particular world for so long, often in positions of responsibility, and because society has been so lapse in supporting more positive role models for both men and women, you work with what you've got, and men's shortcomings in the workplace are a bit more evident.

Nevertheless, sources of gender conflict at work are many. Following are some typical examples:

• Sally and Jean are the only two members of a young design team at a software company that needs to meet a deadline for a new product. It's a tense situation because a lot is riding on the outcome, and everyone in the mix is trying to blast a solution out of the granite of unrealized possibilities. The two women become offended by an increasingly confrontational approach and find themselves out-shouted by the men. They finally give up and acquiesce to whatever decisions their male colleagues make.

• There is one woman in a room full of men, and someone needs to take notes. Everyone occupies an equal position in the company, but who do you think ends up with the job, either voluntarily or by being volunteered?

• Doug and Connie are working on a project together, but it's getting bogged down in details. Doug, frustrated, wants to speed things up, while Connie thinks the solution is to go deeper into the problem until all the options are sorted out. The project stalls as each blames the other for sabotaging the process.

• Your department hires a new female manager who shows favoritism to her male staff while underrating the contributions of the women who report to her. The men go out of their way to gain her approval; the women feel betrayed and angry.

• A male supervisor explains to Fred how a particular task needs to be done, and Fred respectfully follows orders. When a female supervisor offers similar advice a week later on a different project, Fred's face shows tension, and he reluctantly carries out her suggestions.

• Denise, a manager at an office products company, tends to go out of her way to ensure that all team members get the recognition they deserve at the conclusion of successful projects. Her arrogant male counterpart rarely makes such an effort but is promoted that year to a position that could easily have been hers. Denise's boss takes her aside one day and suggests that while "being a good person" is a virtue, it may limit her chances of moving ahead in the company.

This last example is just the outcome that Joyce K. Fletcher, a professor of management at Simmons Graduate School of Management, warns about in her book *Disappearing Acts: Gender, Power, and Relational Practice at Work*. In it she talks about the ideals of what has been called relational theory—empathy, authenticity, vulnerability, mutual empowerment—and how they have the potential to transform our workplaces. Unfortunately, her research has shown that such characteristics, all of which have communication as a key component, are still undervalued in most companies, "dismissed as personal attributes rather than counted as competencies." The result, she concludes, is that the people who come most naturally to these behaviors— women and men who don't fit the alpha male stereotype— are susceptible to a unique kind of discrimination that dismisses the very abilities that are needed in corporate America.

"Those who enable others," she writes, "are likely to be characterized by coworkers as 'helpful' or 'nice' people rather than as competent workers who are contributing to organizational learning.... [Those] who spoke of avoiding conflict in order to create an environment where people would feel free to express their ideas were often characterized not as collaborative team players but as people with dependency issues who were afraid of confrontation because they had a 'need to be liked.'"

Finally, no discussion of gender in the workplace would be complete without mentioning sexual harassment and unequal pay. These are serious issues with a long history of legal and cultural grist behind them. On the surface it seems like a no-brainer to simply eliminate inappropriate behaviors and inequitable wage biases from the workplace, but as everyone knows, these problems are much more complicated and subtler than that. The forces behind them are deeply entrenched, with both natural and "human-made" origins and no easy solutions.

Clearly, the essential natures of man and woman won't change any time soon. Each has been programmed by "God by whatsoever name" and by the society they grew up in to think, act, and communicate in different ways. These differences can lead to conflict, and the workplace is clearly not immune to it. However, certain things *can* be changed, and as you'll read below, improving our communication skills and learning to recognize the patterns and styles of our gender opposites will address many of the problems that have been mentioned in this chapter. As our own self-knowledge and our sensitivity to others grow, we'll begin to translate that awareness into more appropriate responses and behavior.

What Now?

Gender conflict presents us with an opportunity to move past conditioned and stereotyped beliefs about who we are as men and women and into discovering how the strengths of masculine and feminine can be blended in pursuit of common goals. Those goals are both external, such as finishing an important project or preserving workplace harmony, and internal—sowing within yourself the seeds of a whole person. I'm not an advocate of androgyny, which feels more like a science-fiction term for boring, but of making the most of all the tools we have for expressing our highest potential as human beings. That man yelling at you from across the table or the woman who just can't seem to get to the point are, believe it or not, your teachers, and the workplace is your classroom.

Many of the solutions to communication dysfunction between men and women are no different from those we would apply to any interaction we have with someone at work: being honest and focused, kind but firm, respectful but clear of intention, and so on. The closer we get to becoming the kind of people we aspire to be—assuming we have such aspirations—the less likely it is that problems will occur at all.

> Gender conflict presents us with an opportunity to move past conditioned and stereotyped beliefs about who we are as men and women.

So much has to do with monitoring ourselves while being aware of others. The potential for a communication miracle begins in the very moment when we recognize that our message—or the message of another—just isn't getting through. When we respond by adjusting our behavior or our attitude, and when that adjustment is reciprocated, a real breakthrough is made.

Still, every situation is unique, every power dynamic is different, and certain rules apply depending on the circumstance. As you've seen from the discussion above, this is particularly true for the delicate dance between women and men at work.

The following suggestions and ideas, then, are offered as a starting point for learning more about the steps to that dance. They won't prevent all the trouble that men and women can get into while working together, but they should get you thinking. More information on how to communicate better at work—equally vital but applicable to both men and women—will be shared in subsequent chapters.

Mostly for Women

In a lot of ways, women are in the driver's seat at work. They are taking up more space in the workforce, the numbers of women-owned companies and women CEOs are on the rise, women are influencing the kinds of benefits that companies provide their employees, such as maternity leave and child care, and qualities that have typically been associated with being female are finding new appreciation in what has formerly been a man's world—business.

Still, complications remain. The "glass ceiling" is a very real phenomenon for many ambitious women who want the same opportunities as their male counterparts. Too often they are the victims of "pipelining," being directed toward such "people-oriented" departments as marketing, personnel, and public relations, those that rarely lead to the upper echelons of an organization. This hasn't stopped them from bowing to existing rules of advancement, but trying to beat men at their own game—understandable under the circumstances—only perpetuates the workplace bias that that favors masculine behavior. I believe corporate cultures must continue to adapt to the more feminine talents of women, not the other way around, and that there are things that a woman can do to bring about a necessary balance while facilitating workplace harmony. Following are just a few:

1. Up to a point it's OK to be "just like a man," but not a primitive one. Be willing to exercise assertiveness, but don't try to out-shout them or arm wrestle them or punish them for being bad. Stand your ground in the truth that you know, and sooner or later others will acknowledge the validity of your point of view. I like this quote from a woman executive who was interviewed by a major business magazine: "I'd rather

persuade people with my powers of reasoning than dictate to them from a higher position."

2. Business is business, and that means decisions must be made and actions taken. Men can sometimes trample others in their often military-like quest for solutions, but the willingness to be decisive does have a place in successful companies. Respecting this tendency in problem-solving settings will give you more room to participate and even to alter that process. And sometimes it's better to just roll the dice than wait for everything to be known—sometimes.

3. The intimacy needs of women are different from those of men, even at work, which can create a variety of problems. Learn to accept a little conflict in the process of coming to a decision. Two men can trash each other all day and still end up in a bar sharing a beer. Don't take things too personally. People can agree to disagree and still get along.

4. Know that many men have much less patience for conversation than many women. This puts the burden on you, who sees dialogue as a tool to make connections, build relationships, and explore options. Try to find a middle ground. Also, watch for verbal and non-verbal clues to how you are—or aren't—being heard. Get your facts lined up before you sit down in a meeting. In groups, speak up when you have a point to

make, but don't get caught up in conversational escalation (as men are wont to do) if your voice is getting lost. Persevere, bang a cup on the table if you need to, but always try to stay within yourself.

5. Don't be afraid to confront inappropriate behavior, whether it be patronizing, sexual, dismissive, and so on. Take time to gather yourself, and then be firm and clear. Ask for support from others. Your honesty may not sit well at first, but you'll be respected for it by other women and also by men who are willing to hear the truth in what you say.

6. Honor your impulses to be a connector. Such skills as listening, facilitating, and supporting are much needed in today's workplace, and hopefully your actions will give men permission to start exercising their own similar abilities.

Mostly for Men

Yes, the business of business is competition, and things usually need to be done "yesterday," but that's no excuse for some of the behaviors that have typically characterized men at work. As we saw in chapter 1, a company's mission does not have to be carried out on a bloodied field of battle; there are many ways to get the job done while preserving a level of common humanity and decency.

At the same time, I know too well the pressures men have grown up with to look good, get ahead, and then defend their turf, and these are difficult things to shake off. But in the new world of business those qualities are becoming less valuable. We are entering an era of relationship building, a time when it's more effective to work with others rather than against them. And no matter how committed your company is—or isn't—to embracing this new way, it's ultimately up to you to be a catalyst, if not for your employer than for yourself and for your colleagues. To that end, I offer these guidelines:

1. In situations where conflict or tensions surface, the first question to ask is, Am I being a jerk? I say that only somewhat facetiously, since often enough men *are* being jerks. (True, women can be jerks too, but historically the term has been more closely associated with men.) Considered from a different angle, the question becomes: Is it me or is it her/them? Take a moment to get a sense of yourself and the situation. What are you feeling—angry, hurt, threatened? Is your voice getting louder; are you interrupting? Step back if you can, take a few deep breaths, return to your center, and reassess. Is there a better way to approach this situation? Can you see conversation as a way to connect and not compete? Sometimes all it takes is validating—not necessarily agreeing with—

another person's point of view to keep things moving in the right direction. Try to bring more patience to the process.

2. Examine your beliefs about women on the job. Do you treat them as equals, or do your thoughts, words, and/or actions reveal a more patronizing attitude? Do you think of women as weaker, as sex objects, as less capable than men?

3. Don't be afraid to ask questions, to "not know it all." This attitude often becomes the opening door to a productive relationship. People generally like to help, and showing some vulnerability gives them the permission to do the same. This is especially important with many women, who place high value on the quality of the connection they have with others. The payoff will be trust, which is as valuable as gold in the workplace.

4. Don't be afraid to share power. Remember, working together is considered a good thing in the new age of business. This doesn't mean you have to subvert your leadership skills, only to exercise them differently.

5. Recent studies have found that when a man exhibits such qualities as strength and assertiveness, he gets favorable marks from his superiors. When a woman shows such behavior, she is regarded with suspicion. The very norms she's expected to meet on the job are

often in conflict with those she's still expected to meet as a woman. Are you guilty of perpetuating such a double standard? Are you gender blind when assessing the performance of others?

6. Ego is good, but too much ego is not. And when too much ego gets associated with your work, priorities become distorted and unhealthy behaviors surface. Be proud of what you do, but be willing to let go and be flexible, to serve the greater good. You are not your job; you are much more than your job. If, for example, a woman—or anyone, for that matter—has a better idea than you do, support it.

7. Just say no to inappropriate comments about a woman's looks. Yes, there is sexual energy in the workplace, but deal with it from a place of respect and sensitivity. Whatever frustrations you're experiencing in your personal life have nothing to do with your female coworkers. Besides, nice guys don't always finish last.

The Best of Both Worlds

Men and women still have a lot to learn from each other, and the workplace is a good place to do it. Each brings a unique set of behaviors and attitudes to their jobs—some of which are learned and some of which are basic to their character. Each is necessary to meet the kinds of challenges that the workplace offers. What's missing is a healthy balance and a comfortable commingling of the two energies, the masculine and the feminine. These energies tend to compete rather than work in tandem, and when that happens the masculine usually triumphs because the workplace has favored that approach. I don't believe this dynamic serves the long-term interests of either companies or the people who work there. Fortunately, it doesn't need to be this way. As both men and women become more aware of the gender patterning of their behaviors at work and seek a balance, so too will the workplace begin to change.

CHAPTER 4

"Listening . . . means taking a vigorous, human interest in what is being told us. You can listen like a blank wall or like a splendid auditorium where every sound comes back fuller and richer."

—ALICE DUER MILLER,
early twentieth-century
American poet/writer

"If you treat [people] the way they are, you never improve them. If you treat them the way you want them to be, you do."

—GOETHE

Getting Along
with Coworkers

I hope that by now you're beginning to understand why something as "simple" as an interaction between two people at work can deteriorate into a tangle of misunderstanding and bad feelings. At any one time we have to contend with our conditioning as males and females, corporate atmospheres of trust or mistrust, our own unique biases and fears: the list goes on. If we aren't aware of at least some of these energies, then even our best intentions to communicate well can fail. So it's imperative that we overcome these influences and concentrate on making good connections with the people with whom we work day in and day out—our coworkers—which is the focus of this chapter. It takes a lot less energy to prevent problems when they surface than to avoid or deny or to keep repeating what remains unresolved.

This isn't about the kibitzing or complaining or socializing that is a natural part of any workplace. We need to make contact and share stories and process frustrations as part of communal and working life. The problem arises when one person is willing and the other isn't, when complaining becomes the norm and substitutes for true problem solving,

or when an interaction between colleagues crosses the sometimes blurry line from normal and healthy to dysfunctional,
destabilizing, or simply nonproductive. Often problems
come up when there's no communication at all, or at least
nothing of any substance. A work environment can be filled
with illusions (for example, "We get along great here") that
are covered up by good manners.

"I like my job well enough," says a high school teacher I
know. "The students are wonderful, and there's always
something interesting going on. But sometimes I'm a little
uncomfortable with the other teachers, and I think they feel
it too. It's like, outwardly there is respect and civility—we're
usually pretty nice to each other—but it's tenuous and can
change abruptly if there's a conflict or a problem. The mood
in the lounge will get tense, and sometimes people will whis-
per. We don't have any easy way to talk about things. Mostly
we just hope they go away."

There are also situations in which someone has made you
a target for their frustrations. An office worker I'll call Jane
laments on an Internet bulletin board ("Disgruntled Workers" at MSN.com) that "there's this woman who keeps
telling everyone my business. It's not mistakes that I have
done. It's things I haven't done yet [like] 'she still hasn't
turned in that report' even though the report isn't due for
another week. It exasperates me. . . . I don't know whether to
confront her—which would probably create even *more*
unjustified gossip about me—or what?"

Jane had apparently landed a management job and the person maligning her hadn't, and she wondered if that had something to do with all the backstabbing and sabotage. Perhaps, but people like that are always looking for scapegoats, and if it wasn't Jane it would be someone else, and if it wasn't because she had lost out on a management job, then it would be for some other reason. Her pent-up anger could have many sources, the most important of which may have nothing to do with work. We may never discover what's behind a coworker's antagonistic behavior, and yet we still need to protect ourselves and communicate our desire for it to stop if it's making our lives difficult.

Identifying Root Causes

Basic disagreements about a particular course of action at work are natural enough, but when they don't get resolved or they escalate into something more personal, then there may be something deeper going on. Think about the last time you had a disagreement or an uncomfortable moment with a coworker. What was it about? Did it ever get resolved? If so, do you feel better about this person as a result? If not, why not? If the problem didn't get settled, what happened?

In many of these tough situations, a primary conflict—often unacknowledged—is getting in the way of effective working relations. I've organized them into several categories.

Personality Differences

This category includes the relationships we tend to describe with such statements as, "I just don't get that guy" or "We aren't on the same wavelength" or "We just don't speak the same language." It includes the many reasons—some obvious and some subtle—that two people can't seem to find a comfortable way to connect with each other. There is an entire field of study that focuses on personality analysis and career compatibility and their use in the workplace. Meyers-Briggs is the most popular and longest-running analysis tool, but there's the Big Five, DiSC, and other profiling systems that have evolved from various research efforts. All of them try to fit individual personalities into a dominant—though not exclusive—type (for example, Thinker, Achiever, Intuitive, Skeptic, Peacemaker, Extrovert), and the results can be very useful for evaluating someone's fit for a particular company or how well a group of people on a given team may get along. Personality differences are a kind of Venus and Mars in the workplace, but all the planets are involved, and probably some nearby galaxies as well.

> Personality differences are a kind of Venus and Mars in the workplace, but all the planets are involved, and probably some nearby galaxies as well.

Style Differences

Related to the above category, we often make judgments about someone's character or motives (as they will about us) based on the *way* that they communicate. For example, if they tend to talk rapidly or loudly or in a high voice, we may think them pushy or arrogant or unwilling to listen to others. Those who are slow talking may be considered slow thinking. We are naturally more comfortable with some communication styles than we are with others. For example, gregarious communication styles—the sociable salesperson type—may work for some, while others may prefer a more quietly attentive and sympathetic style. We thus tend to avoid or diminish people whose styles we don't like, even if that person has much of value to offer us.

Cultural Differences

Problems provoked by cultural differences are bound to increase as the U.S. workforce becomes even more diverse and global, because many people just aren't comfortable working with members of other races and cultures. Our assumptions about the behaviors and attitudes of other "tribes" affects how we see and treat such people. At his website LifeintheUSA.com, Elliot Essman advises newly hired foreign workers, "Making yourself comfortable in the workplace environment once you have a job will probably be the toughest adjustment you'll have to make in America.... Your first safe assumption about your American coworkers is that they either will know nothing about the country you come from or be seriously misinformed about it based on bits and pieces they've seen on television." And how many times has the same thing been true from their side, that our friends from other countries get their first impression of us from the media and pop-culture imagery and the fast-food icons with which they're inundated in their homeland?

Dr. Milton Bennett of the Intercultural Communication Institute has developed what he calls the Development Model of Intercultural Sensitivity (DMIS), which shows the stages that people go through as they adjust toward those different from them. First there is *denial* (failure to recognize real differences), then *defense* (overprotection of one's own cultural identity), *minimization* (assumption that differences are small and that others can/should become more like us), *acceptance* (belief that we are just one of many equally complex cultures), *adaptation* (ability to see the world through different eyes and to alter our behavior to improve communication), and *integration* (similar to adaptation, the ability to move in and out of other worldviews, as do expatriates or "global nomads").

Ego Problems

Problems of the ego are a little easier to pin down. They arise when one person or another (or both) chooses his or her own perception of reality as the ultimate truth of a situation rather than open up to other perspectives. This is usually a defensive posture, motivated by fear or ambition or insecurity—whenever we feel our self-concept is at risk. We become attached to a particular outcome or point of view not so much because we believe that it's right (which can turn out to be true) but because it represents an extension of who we are—or who we have come to believe we are. If it's rejected, no matter the reason, it means that *we* have been rejected, and that's not OK. So our egos fight for validation, not for the best course of action.

Trust Issues

Many believe that trust is at the bottom of most communication and relationship issues at work (and everywhere else). The extent to which we trust another person to respect who we are *and* our point of view makes us that much more willing to open ourselves up to them in a spirit of goodwill and collaboration. A lack of trust, on the other hand, comes from a sense that we aren't being respected or that the other person wants to control or manipulate us. In such cases we withdraw, hold back what we know, protect ourselves, or fight back.

Misuse of Power

Power is misused most often when there is a clear hierarchical relationship involved, such as between a manager and those she or he manages. (This issue will be addressed in greater depth in chapter 5, which focuses on the manager-managed dynamic.) Yet even among peers there can be instances when someone has been assigned or has volunteered for temporary control of a project and then uses that position for revenge, personal gain, or some other reason that is threatening or hurtful to others. There are also those who use their specialized knowledge as a way to have power over others. Then there are the bullies, those whose "power-over" personalities prey on others' vulnerabilities. These troubled souls are usually in pain, but it's a pain they don't want to feel, so they take it out on others. They have no respect for others or themselves, and trust scares them to death. They also have lots of strategies for denying their hurt and their hurtful actions.

Committing to Communication Excellence

Despite the variety of reasons for communication breakdowns in the workplace, I believe that the solution to most of them starts with each of us and the promises we make to ourselves to approach things differently. Yes, we can use many specific behaviors and strategies, and several are offered in the section below. Here, however, I'm talking about the basic assumptions that underlie what we do. For example, if I assume that the company I'm working for will soon go out of business, then I probably won't make more than a minimum effort while I circulate my resume throughout the land. If, on the other hand, I think the company has a lot of promise and I want to stay there, then my attitude and actions will reflect that belief.

The same is true when we think about how to get along with others—in this case our coworkers—but it really applies across the board. If we don't really care about the outcome, if we've settled on the notion that one way or the other things will get done and, hey, it's just a job, then these attitudes will influence our behavior. And, sometimes that's an adequate response. If, on the other hand, we make those interactions part of a bigger picture that places a high value on positive outcomes, then we'll start approaching them in a spirit that reflects that desire.

And so the best way to start improving your communication effectiveness at work is to make it a priority to do so, guided by a few simple commitments that you can make to yourself:

I commit to the value of building good relationships at work. Strong relationships are at the center of most harmonious workplaces. The more comfortable you are with someone, the easier it is to share thoughts and opinions without fear of conflict. Sometimes these relationships fall into place easily, such as with people with whom you feel a natural affinity. Other times it's a struggle to make even a tolerable connection with another person, and it can seem like too much effort for too little payoff.

But even if you aren't looking for a best friend at work,

> The best way to start improving your communication effectiveness at work is to make it a priority to do so.

fostering cooperative relationships can pay off in many ways. I've always wanted to get along with my coworkers. I may not especially like someone, I may not make plans to see them on the weekend, but our paths will cross frequently during any given day, and I want those instances to at least be productive. Sometimes it doesn't take much more than a smile or a shared joke or showing appreciation for something someone did to help create a bond, however brief it may be. If, on the other hand, you feel that the people around you are a drain or see human contact as a necessary evil, then over time you'll start to isolate yourself. Your productivity may suffer, and your job will become merely something to endure. Relationship building is a vital element of a healthy workplace and an important means of staying meaningfully connected with the world around us.

I commit to communicating better with others. This isn't as easy as it sounds. Why bother trying to work things out with someone whom you wish would get transferred to the office in northern Alaska? As someone wrote on an MSN.com workplace bulletin board, "There are just too many rude and inconsiderate people out there, and that's hard enough to deal with every day, but when they come into your workplace, or worse yet—work in your workplace—you can't get away from them." Since you only see these people at work, what's the point of trying? Spend as little time with them as you must, do what you have to do, and then it's over. Right? In a way, though, the frustrated Internet poster answered her own question. These people *won't* go away; they are on your team whether you like it or not, so you may as well get used to it and try to make any interaction as pleasant as you can, not so much for their benefit but for yours.

More important, committing to be a better communicator will make your job easier, and who doesn't want that? Lots of things are going on at work all the time—decisions, deadlines, meetings, and so on—so you're in constant contact with your colleagues. The better you are at communicating clearly and listening effectively, at keeping your balance when the boat is rocking, the more likely your stress levels will drop and the outcomes you seek will be reached. You will also feel better inside, because you'll have connected with others in a more authentic way while giving them the chance to respond in kind.

I commit to believing that most people want to get along and will do the right thing if given a chance. I think that most of us want to feel good about ourselves and be perceived by others as decent people. This doesn't prevent us from doing the wrong thing sometimes, because, after all, we are complicated beings, with a chaotic mix of thoughts and feelings tumbling around inside us. But who wants to go home after a long day at the office and keep replaying a scene that turned out bad or left hurt feelings or will be waiting for you in the morning? How would you feel if you found out that you'd offended someone or had a reputation as a difficult person? Probably not so great, and you'd want to do something about it. Now assume that your coworkers are equally

> We generally behave as if ours is the only reality that counts and then wonder why we're having so much trouble getting along with others.

sensitive, and you'll start to create a space in which problem solving can occur.

I commit to looking at each interaction with coworkers as a learning opportunity and not as a test of right or wrong. In the heat of a difficult moment with another we often forget how similar we are to that person, not so much in terms of personality, which we know can take countless shapes, but in the ways in which we each operate from a reality of our own making. The only world we have ever experienced is the one seen through our own eyes and felt in our own bones. In fact, we generally behave as if ours is the only reality that counts and then wonder why we're having so much trouble getting along with others.

The idea of approaching work as a learning environment is vitally important. It's been said that there are three areas of knowledge:

1. What you know

2. What you know you don't know (but you know where to find out)

3. What you don't know you don't know (by far the largest area of the three)

At work there is much we don't know, but much we assume or don't even realize is worth knowing. When two or more people are trying to achieve a common goal, this ignorance can easily lead to misunderstanding, frustration, and anger. Organizational psychologist Ronald Short explained this predicament well in his book *Learning in Relationship:*

> You share a basic dilemma with everybody else on the planet. You live a rich life inside your head. You continually react, interpret, infer, and provide meaning to what happens to you. You create, author, edit, produce, direct and act in your own internal drama. Others can't know what goes on inside you unless you tell them, but they often *assume* they do—so they don't ask.
>
> Others have rich lives inside their heads as well. They also react, interpret, infer, and provide meaning to what happens to them. You can't know what it is unless they tell you, but you often *assume* you do—so you don't inquire.
>
> Everything flows from these simple facts.

As Dr. Short sees it, most of the problems that occur at work can be traced not to ill-intentioned people but to "interactions that produce missing, misattributed, misinterpreted information." Many of our interactions at work are a collision of agendas and set beliefs about the nature of a situation. We simply don't have the skills or awareness—or often the time—to sort them all out and choose the most satisfying solutions. But we need to start making the time and building those tools of inquiry. Without stepping back and looking at an issue with fresh eyes, with "beginner's mind" (as a Zen practitioner might call it), we can lose our perspective and waste precious time hassling over things that really aren't very important.

I commit to taking risks. Someone has to take the first step in building a good relationship with another, and it may have to be you! Opening yourself to someone when you're unsure of his or her motives or of your own ability to connect is certainly a scary thing, and in fact I don't recommend charging into the void like a garrulous Don Quixote. We are fragile creatures, after all, vulnerable to the slings and arrows of insensitive souls. Nevertheless, once you start the process, you will often be amazed at what happens.

I can recall a situation with two female colleagues who simply rubbed each other the wrong way. They had known each other for years, had had their share of ups and downs, but inevitably they ended up in the downs, and it was taxing not only on them but also on those with whom they worked. One day the two of them sat down—with me in the middle—and decided to throw it all on the table. No one wanted to speak at first, and the first words that came out were tense and blaming and angry. But we persisted, and by the end of the two-hour meeting the energy in the room had changed completely. The two coworkers discovered that each had vulnerabilities and that each had some good points to make about the other. They didn't necessarily like what they heard, but they listened nonetheless and learned from it.

And so taking a risk invites transformation. When we keep things bottled up inside, they have no place to go but round and round and round, like rats in a maze. There are safe ways of sharing real feelings with a coworker, and while you may not always get back what you hoped for, you may get back even more than you expected, and in any case you'll feel better for having made the effort. Indeed, when you commit to communication effectiveness at work, you'll find that the very act of putting yourself out there is often the greatest reward.

By the way, it does helps the commitment process if you value the company you work for and want to continue working there. Such loyalty is an excellent motivator for putting all of who you are into your work. Not only will you benefit, but your employer will as well. If you believe in that company and its mission and the way its treats the people who work there, then nurturing your workplace relationships is a wonderful way of giving something back. This is where the idea of community comes in, the sense that everyone is in this thing together. The closer you feel to the people you work with, the more successful the entire effort will be. But even if you have no particular loyalty to your workplace, improving your communication skills will help you while you're there and follow you wherever you go.

Six Steps to a Communication Miracle

The art and science of good communication is a combination of self-assessment and situational assessment. It's about paying attention to what is going on inside you and being aware of what is happening outside you. It's about being absolutely present in the moment, in the now. Yes, the past will influence how you might respond in the present; it will provide information that you may be able to use. And the future will always be tugging at you, trying to make sure its needs are factored into any decision making equation. But the immediate moment is where the action is, where the energy is live, and where things are happening, literally as you speak. It is in that spirit that I offer the following tools and tips. They are designed to help create a space where two or more people can communicate effectively and deal with most any conflict or situation that arises.

Think of yourself as an explorer and the world of communication as a largely unmapped territory. You've committed to the journey, and now it begins to get interesting.

1. Establish Trust

The first step in building a bridge to another person is to prove that she or he can trust you to be a decent human being and to make thoughtful decisions. At work, this means respecting confidences (for example, not gossiping about a coworker's life or "letting something slip" to a supervisor), offering constructive feedback—not criticism—

honoring your responsibilities, and being available if someone needs support. If you truly want to connect with a coworker in a real and productive way, you will do well to approach them with your palms open and your agenda clear.

Consider this scenario: You're at your desk and a colleague bursts in. You know he's working on a big project with a deadline up ahead, and you are one of several people who has information that he needs. He's a nitpicker when it comes to statistics and can be harsh if something seems off. He also wants it "yesterday" but won't actually admit it, preferring instead to make vague references to how swamped and pressured he is. Another person comes in later—knocking first—with a similar request. She realizes how tough it is to get certain numbers right and is willing to work with what you've got and deal with any gaps if they come up. She tells you up front that she needs the information for a meeting in two days and asks if that will be a problem.

What emotions does each scenario bring up in you? Which one of these people would you rather work with? Who will you go out of your way to help out? The nitpicker is being vague about his needs

> The first step in building a bridge to another person is to prove that she or he can trust you to be a decent human being and to make thoughtful decisions.

while using a thinly veiled threat (with a little martyrdom thrown in) to motivate you to help him. He isn't respecting your situation, and his questionable way of getting what he wants doesn't inspire trust. The other colleague puts you at ease right away by letting you know that she's sensitive to your job demands. She tells you exactly what she needs and when she needs it and then offers to work out a plan that addresses both of your concerns.

When it comes to gaining another's confidence, there's no substitute for speaking honestly, showing respect, and being forthright with what you know. For communication to flow smoothly between two people there has to be a feeling of safety. As most of us know, such trust can take time to develop; we've had bad experiences in the past and need reassurance. Our job as communication masters-in-training is to be patient and to keep looking for opportunities, however small, to start building those bridges of trust.

2. Check for Unfinished Business

Good intentions can be sabotaged if we have unresolved issues with the person with whom we're trying to communicate—in other words, we can't really start with a clean slate unless we have a clean slate. If you're still dealing with the negative fallout from a specific event—say, this coworker never did acknowledge your help on a recent project—then you'll have trouble approaching her in a helpful, team-building spirit because your resentment and hurt have never been addressed. It doesn't have to be a gross infraction to keep you from being open, just large enough to distract you from giving the interaction your all.

Basically, you can do one of two things: You can bring up your discomfort with that person, explaining what it is and how it affects your ability to work with her in the present (using the various communication tools presented throughout this book), or you can process the feeling without her and clean the slate yourself. In the first instance, you need to feel secure enough in who you are that such truth-telling doesn't make you too vulnerable; just because you are being honest about addressing a problem doesn't mean that the other person will respond in kind. She may get defensive no matter how diplomatic you are, she may see the situation totally differently, or she may not see a problem at all. Be prepared for anything.

Start the conversation with something like, "There's a situation that's been bothering me, and I feel uncomfortable talking about it, but I want to get it behind me. It has to do with that project we were on last week." Stick to your truth and try not to blame. Figure out beforehand what you need from the person—an apology or an explanation. Let her know it's important to you because you're going to be working with her and you don't want the past to get in the way.

The second approach is emotionally safer but requires different skills. In this case, you figure out exactly what bothers you the most about this person or about what happened between the two of you. Is it something she did, a style she has, a personality you don't like? Then a good question to ask is, "Is this something I can let go? Is it worth spending more of my energy on?" Most of the time the answer will be no. I think of how author Richard Carlson popularized the axiom, "Don't sweat the small stuff, and it's all small stuff." Well, maybe not *all* of it, but most of it surely is. Again, you're not making this effort for the other person's benefit but for *your* benefit. If you've done your inner work and there's still something that you can't completely excuse or forget, then you may have to go to that person and tell her your concerns. If it's a really sticky issue and the situation gets too difficult, consider asking a neutral third party, such as a respected coworker or a well-liked manager, to sit in on the process.

3. Communicate Your Intent to Learn

The commitment to seeing all interactions as opportunities for learning will lead to an entirely new way of communicating with your colleagues. You'll no longer prioritize your own version of reality but instead see it as part of a bigger picture, communicating that awareness with words and actions that the other person understands. Most people, used to defending their point of view, will be surprised when someone makes an effort to really understand them. The beauty of this dynamic is that as your coworker responds to your intent to learn, he or she will be more willing to learn about *your* position. This give-and-take is at the heart of the learning process. The objective is finding common ground at the highest level you can get to.

A variety of communication techniques can be used to guarantee that everything that needs to be said is said—*and* understood. These include questions meant to clarify ("What did you mean by..." or "Can you say it another way?"); to explore ("How do you see...?" or "What is most important to you about...?"); to summarize ("Let me see if I got this right..." or "So what you're saying is..."); to validate ("I'm with you..." or "I understand"); and to confirm ("Are you okay with this decision?" or "Are we in agreement here?").

It's also important to let the other person know that disagreement is OK and that you're willing to open your perspective to new and better ideas. Conflict, engaged in respectfully and even passionately, is a potent way to get down to what's most important. And "constructive feedback"—pointing out to each other both the strengths and weaknesses of an argument or a behavior—is an excellent learning tool if delivered without judgment and if the receiver is open to hearing it. All of these techniques are invitations to a two-way conversation, to a process of mutual discovery. They also help to establish an atmosphere of trust and respect, because you're telling the other person that you need and value their input, that in fact you can't reach a solution without them.

One thing to watch for is getting sucked back in to your attachment to a preferred outcome or belief. You've been snagged when you find yourself pushing too hard or talking too loud or listening too little while your conversational dance partner is responding in the same way. You'll both end up ignoring signs that your message isn't getting through, which you'll ironically interpret to mean that you must carry on even more vigorously. The result: Nothing new is being learned, but there's quite a lot of activity.

4. Listen Carefully

I read somewhere that if you learn to do only one thing well when it comes to communication, it should be to listen, to really listen. When you give your full attention to someone, you give him confidence that you're really there to hear him, and he'll just keep opening up like a flower in spring. You'll also discover that there's a lot more information to work with than you ever thought possible: choice of words, nuances of voice, body language, all this and more suddenly yield their secrets to you. And as they do, both the content and intent of what the person is telling you become clearer, and your response that much more appropriate and constructive.

One big clue that we aren't really focused on what someone is saying is how quickly we respond after he has finished speaking. When a person is talking, it doesn't mean we use that time to figure out what to say next. It's just the opposite; we use that time to listen. Then by waiting a few beats after after that person has finished, especially when the subject matter is complex or highly charged, we give ourselves an extra moment to compose our thoughts and respond with a higher degree of sensitivity.

This skill doesn't happen overnight, though; to hone it takes willingness, practice, and patience. Developing this skill means that your own vulnerabilities may also be exposed as the conversation deepens. It means that you must learn to put your needs and biases

> If you learn to do only one thing well when it comes to communication, it should be to listen, to really listen.

aside, at least for a while, which is no easy task. Those biases are strong, and they can cut you off from hearing important truths. For example, let's say you've concluded that Gary hasn't been handling a client you used to manage as well as he should be. This client is coming into the office tomorrow, and Gary is talking to you about how best to deal with her. Because of your preconceived belief about who Gary is (someone who can't be trusted to do the right thing with this client), you may dismiss his ideas (by not listening well) when in fact he may have valuable insights to share.

Careful listening can also be sidetracked by other distractions that creep into a conversation: boredom, overload, stress, your own demanding priorities, as well as problems you have with *how* that person is communicating with you. Learning to listen well is a real challenge, but the effort to master this skill will pay off, for you and for your coworker.

5. Watch Your Language

Much of what we're talking about here involves some fairly

sensitive areas. We're asking each other to open up, to trust in a process with which few will be familiar or comfortable. How we say what we want to say is thus a vital component of any successful communication. "You're really a kick-ass saleswoman!" bellowed from across the room won't have the same effect as looking that same person straight in the eye and telling her with obvious respect (and hopefully in a lower voice) the same thing.

And so we need to be aware of the words we use and the effect they have on people. Much has been said, for example, of "I" statements versus "you" statements. Which would you rather hear: "You were really late with that report. You screwed up my whole day" or "It's too bad the report was late. I had to change my schedule to fit it in." The first one puts me on the defensive, and I'll probably sink into guilt or maybe get angry because it feels like a parental scolding. The second one gives me room for my emotions, and I'll be much more likely to acknowledge the problems I created for the other person. The first statement may feel righteous to the "injured" party, but it probably won't lead to problem solving. The second one is harder to say because the same emotional conflict may exist, but it does create more options for dealing with what happened. The risk the second person takes is that I—Mr. Late Report—will take advantage of his diplomatic response by minimizing what I did or avoiding responsibility. If I do, then I will have missed a safe opportunity to be honest about what happened, and my colleague won't be so generous the next time.

Be aware, too, that certain words and phrases are guaranteed communication landmines. Sentences that begin with or include such modifiers as "but," "no," "don't," "should," "can't," and so on will often lead to a defensive or even an offensive response, pushing the conversation into rougher waters. Try to find more sensitive ways to communicate a concern or a difference in opinion.

6. Deal with Emotions

OK, all these things sound wise and practical, but what if an emotional trigger has been pulled? How can you be a communication maestro if all you really want to do is punch someone in the nose? It's a fair question, and indeed if our communication skills are to be improved, we need to pay attention to our emotional reality.

In chapter 2 we talked a lot about why anger and fear are so prevalent in the workplace, how the stress of too much work and insensitive bosses and rude people and dysfunctional companies can drive any of us over the edge. We talked about being honest about our feelings and attending to our pain, and about the value of detachment and analysis and putting our emotions into perspective. If we don't attend to those needs, if we're unhappy or stressed or struggling with painful feelings, then there's little chance we'll ever be able to communicate effectively. And so deal with them we must, if not for the company's sake, then for our own.

Science writer and psychologist Daniel Goleman has written and spoken at length about what earlier researchers called "emotional intelligence" (EI). EI basically describes the ability of someone to recognize and regulate emotions in themselves and even in others. This ability includes such things as knowing how our emotions may be affecting our work performance, linking specific emotions to specific thoughts or people or situations, managing impulsive feelings, not letting strong emotions stop us from thinking, and recognizing the emotional messages of others. The value of EI in the workplace is rising, and for good reason.

When strong emotions do come up, there are several ways to handle them. As explained earlier in the second step to a communication miracle, you can share the feeling with your conversational partner without blaming or attacking. You can do this immediately or wait until you've had time to examine the experience more closely. Know that you have a right to your feelings, but know too that dumping them on another isn't appropriate.

You can also process your emotions internally. One method open to variation is called Freeze-Frame®, developed by Doc Lou Childre. When you recognize a stressful feeling, you "freeze frame" it right away, which basically means putting it in a box and taking a time-out to look at. You then shift your attention to your heart, breathing and focusing there for ten seconds. Try to recall a positive feeling or experience. Ask your heart how best to respond to what happened, then listen for an answer. The things to remember about this approach to managing your emotions are the value of stepping away to get a bigger perspective and create a space for change and the importance of steady breathing, which will naturally slow things down.

What if someone else loses their cool? The most important thing you can do is to not lose yours; it will only make things worse. Try to separate the content or intention of his communication—what he's trying to say to you—from whatever emotion may be attached to it. Don't be unsympathetic; it's fine to acknowledge what he's feeling ("I can see that you're really upset by Sue's comment"), and, in fact, empathy and compassion may be just what someone needs. But don't let his discomfort become your discomfort.

A note about bullies: If a bully has singled you out for torment, it can be hard to ignore him or her. Since bullies' "power-over" personalities thrive on their target's defensiveness, try not to give them any energy. The best communication in this case might be no communication at all. Some will get bored and simply go away. Also, if you can see the smallness of their actions as a sign of weakness, or if you can picture them as some pompous cartoon character, then they'll start to look less threatening. The more malicious and persistent people will require stronger medicine. Sometimes it's best to take a deep breath, find your inner strength, then confront them and draw some hard boundaries. An "I will not accept this kind of treatment" approach may not stop them in their tracks, but most bullies don't expect people to stand up to them. In fact, your resistance may be just the wake-up call they need to realize that they've become someone they really don't want to be.

With tougher cases, you may be forced to take your concerns to someone with authority such as a sympathetic supervisor. Document the bully's behavior, and ask others for their experiences and their support if they seem open to giving it. If someone is picking on you, he or she will probably be targeting others as well, and that won't be good for business.

Follow-Through and Beyond

The above six steps offer a blueprint for transforming your interactions with your coworkers. They aren't to be followed sequentially, of course; ideally they will be happening simultaneously as you engage someone in conversation, assess what is trying to happen, stay tuned to both your and the other person's needs, and make adjustments as you go. There will always be twenty-twenty hindsight: "Gosh, I wish I hadn't said that" or "I just figured out what he meant by...." But once you've made a good connection with someone, you can always go back and fill in the gaps.

In fact, a key part of effective communication is setting the stage for whatever needs to happen next. When you and your coworker have finished talking about the issue at hand, it's important to summarize any decisions that were made and then to agree on the next steps, if any are necessary. The first part is to make sure that you're both on the same page, that you end with a common understanding. The second is to keep the momentum going if there are still some loose ends. This could include another meeting, more information to be gathered, other people who need to be included in the process, and so on. Postmeeting reminders (e-mail, voice mail, passing by in the hallway) can also be helpful to keep things on track and to stay personally connected.

All the above takes honesty, patience, discernment, self-awareness, and a deep commitment to making communication an active part of a healthy work environment. A colleague and friend of mine talks about the definition of a corporation as a "collection of conversations," both internal (those we have inside ourselves) and external (those we have with others). As you've seen above, both play a role in the struggle to bring sanity to our interactions with others. The more closely aligned they become with each other, the more they reflect the goals of an enlightened communicator, the closer we will get to true workplace harmony.

CHAPTER 5

"Good leaders make people feel that they're at the very heart of things, not at the periphery. Everyone feels that he or she makes a difference to the success of the organization. When that happens, people feel centered and that gives their work meaning."

—WARREN BENNIS

"There is nothing noble about being superior to some other man. The true nobility is in being superior to your previous self."

—HINDU PROVERB

Communicating Up and Down the Ladder

The one area that screams the loudest for enlightened models of workplace communication—and not just models but also courageous people willing to implement them—is management-employee relations. Movies such as *9 to 5* and *Office Space,* along with the popular Dilbert cartoon strip, trumpet the frustrations that beset the difficult dance between those who manage and those who are managed. Most of the bosses depicted in these venues are either foul-tempered primates, Machiavellian backstabbers, or dangerous buffoons. The hapless workers are uniformly taken advantage of, but (at least in the movies) they triumph in the end by asserting their dignity and earning respect while demolishing the pretensions of their tyrant supervisors. It's a common stereotype with roots in reality, but as we shall see, there's enough responsibility to go around when assessing what it will take to turn this situation around.

Nevertheless, available data point to a grim picture of managerial competence and compassion.

• A well-documented 1991 report presented at a conference called "Work and Well-Being: An Agenda for the 1990s" concluded, among other things, that "In study after study, across organizations, geographical locations, and time periods, at least 60 percent of workers surveyed report that the most stressful aspect of their job is their immediate supervisor."

• The results of a nationwide "workplace-values" survey published in 1994 found that while the majority of respondents preferred to be motivated by techniques based on caring and wanted more freedom to express their feelings, corporations tended to use fear to motivate and felt that feelings had no place in the office.

• A 1996 employee survey told a large quasi-governmental organization that more than 50 percent of the people who worked there believed that: 1) management couldn't be expected to do the right thing; 2) management didn't communicate the reasons for its decisions to employees; and 3) employees couldn't speak their minds without fear of reprimand from management. A similar percentage felt that the company didn't empower its employees and did not have a culture based on trust and that workers weren't honest and open with one another.

• Forty-two percent of respondents to an online survey sponsored last year by the Business Research Lab said they had quit a job because they "didn't like the supervisor." Another survey found that when employees do quit, a sobering 85 percent of them are leaving their bosses, not their jobs.

• "Management practice," defined primarily as a supervisor's "interpersonal style"—her or his ability to interact with and effectively lead the people she or he is responsible for—was by a huge margin the most frequently mentioned "undiscussable" at work, as reported by Kathleen D. Ryan and Daniel K. Oestreich in *Driving Fear Out of the Workplace.*

Frank, a grade school teacher, describes his principal as the "worst 'people manager' I've ever experienced in my life. Her manner is truly course and unfriendly. She appears to believe that management is best accomplished through fear and intimidation and uses her position to keep people in place. She is defensive and hostile and doesn't take suggestions in any form. She is a micromanager and never gives the people she manages any real feeling of accomplishment or success. She does not communicate her goals or expectations clearly, leaving most of us in a state of confusion."

There are many who deal with these kinds of frustrations every day; the nature of hierarchical relationships is fraught with dysfunctional potential. On the one hand, there has to be a certain level of "buck stopping" and final decision making for things to get done, and this means that someone has to take on that difficult role. On the other hand, you hope that those in such positions got there because they have the tools and experience to do their jobs well. This often isn't

> The nature of hierarchical relationships is fraught with dysfunction.

the case, however, and you end up with online forums with names like "Disgruntled Workers" and "Office Talk," where people download their grievances about bosses who seem intent on making their lives miserable.

A Tale of Two Realities

Before we get too comfortable laying waste to the management kingdom, though, we need to take a peek at the other side. Think of how a typical six-year-old might describe the management skills of a parent: "Too bossy, doesn't let me do anything I really want to do, hides my chocolates, makes me get up too early in the morning...." Parents, on the other hand, have their own burden to carry: "Whiny, won't listen, thinks he knows everything, room's always a mess, doesn't know what I go through...." I don't mean to suggest that the essence of the manager-managed relationship is one of overbearing adult and petulant child, but in many workplaces that's not an unfair description when things aren't going well. Consider this excerpt from a recent article at Workforce.com called "Building Better Bosses," which begins by asking a technology manager to describe the toughest part of her job: "I think the hardest thing for managers is getting the job done while dealing with different personalities. Some days I feel like I'm baby-sitting." When asked about the most rewarding part of her job, she hesitated. "Can I have more time to think about that question?"

In my own experience as a manager, albeit in small companies, I can attest to the challenges of handling a disparate group of people with different needs and different skill levels. I had to monitor performance, give feedback, address defensiveness, rectify mistakes, facilitate disputes, hire and let go—all the while meeting my own deadlines and answering to my boss. Most managers are employees themselves, and while they do have more power than those "below" them, they also have more responsibilities and different, sometimes more difficult, demands.

Most managers are in fact under tremendous pressure to get things done, and many have less support than those they manage. The American Management Association surveyed nearly one thousand of its members in 2000, asking them to rate what they felt were the most important factors in achieving high-level organizational performance and if managers were competent in those areas. Those showing the biggest gaps between "What we need" and "Are we doing it?" were "coaching and mentoring skills" (a 56 percent difference between "need" and "doing"), "time management" (51 percent), and "listening and asking questions" (47 percent). In other words, managers clearly recognize the value of support systems and of communicating with the intent to learn but admit they haven't been successful in making those priorities a reality. Not having enough time is one of many culprits.

These challenges, however, don't excuse unfair or disrespectful treatment. Of the four skill areas rated in the AMA survey—conceptual skill, effectiveness, communication, and

> Managing others *can* be a fulfilling experience, and being managed *can* be something to rely on, not to brace against.

interpersonal skill—interpersonal skill was rated the lowest in terms of its value to an organization. Nevertheless, one of the responsibilities of those higher on the corporate ladder is to be a role model for the people they manage, exhibiting behaviors and attitudes that inspire others to do their best. In *The Healing Manager: How to Build Quality Relationships and Productive Cultures at Work,* authors William and Kathleen Lundin write that, "A healing manager is a person who helps others grow emotionally and intellectually.... The traits of a healing manager ... [s]tart with an ordinary person who is willing to listen. See that person nod and smile, encouraging additional dialogue. Watch the way that person moves—energetic, well-directed, secure. When someone like that walks into a room, others feel better."

Managing others *can* be a fulfilling experience, and being managed *can* be something to rely on, not to brace against. It all depends on the quality of the relationships that exist between managers and their staffs and on whether hierarchy is used to enable employee performance or protect the status quo. Is communication a two-way affair? Is there mutual support and respect? Is honesty a part of the equation? In decision making is everyone's input valued? If a conscious effort is made to nurture healthy relations—and it does take such a commitment—then bridges will be built and a sense of community will blossom. If, however, everyone has a bunker mentality, then the war will persist and no one wins, least of all the company for which you work.

It's Not Easy Being a Manager (or Being Managed)

There are many reasons why managers and the people they manage have such a tough time getting along. Some of these issues are the same ones that keep coworkers from making healthy connections: personality differences, awkward communication styles, stress, fatigue, problems at home. Unlike the challenges that coworkers face, though, the dynamic between those higher and lower in a workplace hierarchy has its own unique challenges and sources, many of which I've summarized below. If all these challenges are added up, they seem insurmountable. Fortunately, they aren't, but before we consider some solutions let's first explore how relationships and communication between different points on the organizational chart can break down.

Corporate Culture

As we saw in chapter 1, a company's mission, goals, and values, its "way of doing business," have a significant impact on how comfortable its employees feel making meaningful contact with others. Those companies that genuinely encourage an esprit de corps, that value open-door policies and open books and visible interactive management, that have low turnover and a high degree of loyalty, that celebrate triumphs and heal from defeats, will have laid the foundation for healthy communication up and down and across every organizational ladder. On the other hand, those that mistrust the people they hire, that use fear and control to keep people in line, that value numbers and ambition over quality and cooperation, will have created an environment in which resentment and dysfunctional communication are inevitable. As above, so below—if the owners and upper-level managers have taken the low road in shaping the internal contours of their company, that is the tune the middle managers will march to and in turn play for those they manage. Even well-meaning managers will struggle within such a system, caught between the demands of their bosses and the needs of the people they manage.

Power Issues

It's tough to ignore the fact that the person with whom you're communicating, and possibly disagreeing, has some influence over your occupational future. No matter how nice your boss is, how understanding and supportive and willing to listen, you still have the underlying knowledge that he or she has more power than you and can legitimately exercise it at any time and, in some companies, for any reason. This awareness can affect the way we communicate with them because we have more at stake and less ability to control the outcome—your boss usually has the final word and can complicate your work life if he or she chooses to. As a result, we might hold ourselves back, resist showing weakness, or become overly defensive. We may go overboard trying to please our boss or seek to curry favor, "playing up" inappropriately or putting another's work down. We may put our boss on a pedestal, ascribe to him or her qualities that aren't true, and generally forget that bosses, too, are human beings. Dealing with a boss compared to dealing with a coworker is similar to dealing with a parent or a sibling; you approach each one differently, both emotionally and psychologically, and often repeat patterns from childhood. No matter how it plays out, if you're intimidated by those with more power, it will affect how you work and muddle your relationships with those "above" you.

At the same time, it's important to acknowledge that some people with power misuse their power. Either they haven't been properly trained in how to exercise it, or they simply like the feeling it gives them, and fairness is never considered. In a healthy workplace culture, these tendencies are muted by checks and balances built into the system; time-tested procedures handle inappropriate behaviors, no matter at what level. When such channels aren't available, though, power abusers can cause a lot of mischief, and, in some cases, real damage.

The Peter Principle

The Peter Principle, first introduced by USC professor of education Laurence Peter in 1969, is the groundbreaking management theory that people in business tend to rise to the level of their incompetence, that just because someone has been promoted to a managerial position doesn't mean he or she possesses the necessary skills to do it well. Corporate "lifers"—those who stay the course for many years while their colleagues leave for greener pastures—can end up in such positions, rising to the top by the sheer length of their employment, but the phenomenon certainly isn't limited to them. Amy, who worked in the marketing department of a mid-sized wholesale/retail chain, was apparently hip-deep in "Peters":

> My company operated on the principle that if some-one was decent at his job, he was qualified to be a manager, in charge of other people doing that job. There was never any acknowledgment that manag-ing people required a specific skill set and, possibly, some training. Therefore, the company was littered with incompetent and ill-equipped middle- and upper-level managers who spent all their time cover-ing their butts, kissing other people's butts, sur-rounding themselves with people willing to kiss their butts, and in constant fear of anyone they perceived to be "smarter" than they were—particularly subor-dinates—who might jeopardize their positions.

Then there are those who are thrown into positions of greater responsibility out of sudden need or under corporate duress such as during downsizing or when two companies merge. Others may have indeed wanted to move into a higher managerial position but realized once they got there that it's not what they expected, that they really aren't very good at managing. However people get beyond their competence levels, they still have a job to do; the people they manage are relying on them to provide leadership and confidence, to motivate and inspire, or to at least listen to and understand their needs. When almost 1,300 executives were asked in an informal poll what they considered the most important quality to look for when hiring a manager, "ability to motivate employees" was most frequently selected.

As the America Management Assiocation study showed, there is a tremendous need for training and mentoring programs that help new managers learn the skills they need to run their departments effectively and that work to keep good managers on board. When these programs aren't available, both well-meaning managers and their staff do the best they can under difficult circumstances, which sometimes isn't enough to prevent the kinds of problems that can strain relationships and compromise performance.

We Said, They Said

The assumptions that managers and staff make each day about each other's work and each other's attitudes could fill a book all by themselves. These assumptions come in many shapes and sizes and tend to feed off one another. Managers make assumptions about the people they manage and about the very act of managing; employees make assumptions

> The assumptions that managers and staff make each day about each other's work and each other's attitudes could fill a book all by themselves.

about the people they report to and about what they can generally expect from management. Some of these perceptions are rooted in experience; others come from various programming such as business classes and corporate folklore; still others are the result of our own biases and conditioning. Most of them are negative. Our communication styles and strategies usually flow from these beliefs. Ryan and Oestreich, the two authors mentioned above, compiled an excellent list of assumptions made by both managers and employees, which I've summarized below.

Negative Assumptions Managers Make About Employees

- They aren't responsible.
- They only want a paycheck.
- They'll never see the big picture.
- They can't be trusted to follow company policy.

- If I don't stay on top of them they'll goof off, and nothing will get done.

- They demand more benefits but won't work harder to earn them.

- They're capable of dishonesty and sabotage.

Negative Assumptions Employees Make About Managers

- They think we're machines, that we don't have a personal life.

- They're secretive and withhold information; they send mixed messages.

- They're more interested in their own ambitions than in doing the right thing.

- They only pay lip service to our needs.

- They'll take the credit for others' work.

- They micromanage and don't trust that we know what we're doing.

- They play politics and show favoritism.

- They always expect us to do more with less.

- If you show the least bit of smarts, they feel threatened.

The cynicism, resentment, and distrust these beliefs can create and *keep reinforcing* will destroy any openings for honesty and respect in every dealing between the two sides. Such negativity is like a virus; it will infect every level of a company's operations and damage its relationships with customers and stakeholders. A survey of 40,000 Americans taken in the early 1990s (the subject of an out-of-print book called *The Day America Told the Truth*) found that an astounding 93 percent admitted to lying "regularly and habitually" in the workplace.

Lack of Acknowledgment and Support

At a recent medical conference of respiratory therapists, I sat in on a session entitled "Creating Healing Environments in Hospitals." The speaker asked the audience a series of yes/no questions about their work experience and requested that they answer by raising their hands. The most hands went up when attendees were asked if they understood the mission of the organization, if they had adequate support for professional development, and if they knew what was expected of them. The fewest went up—maybe a quarter of the room—when asked if they had received praise in the last seven days or felt that their opinions counted. Different groups of workers will respond in different ways to such questions, of course, but clearly this is a challenge in many workplaces.

Amy recalls a situation in her company when her efforts were slighted, along with those of her colleagues.

> The four coordinators in our department were a pretty qualified bunch. We worked hard. We did

good work. And, to a big extent, we worked independently and somewhat autonomously—each had our "pet" projects and responsibilities. Yet, when discussing each of these projects during a retreat, the marketing director would consistently mention the manager that the project fell under, rather than the coordinator who actually did the work and in most cases had all the information about it.... It simply didn't sit well with me to have someone else be given, and consequently take, credit for my work. And it wasn't just happening to me, it was happening to my coworkers, too.

What We Don't Talk About

We can't ignore the reality that "management practice" (however vaguely defined) is an issue that few people are willing to discuss. To deny that a manager's behavior or lack of skills is having a negative impact on employee performance and corporate health is both counterintuitive and symptomatic of a dysfunctional workplace. But climates of fear and mistrust do exist in the places we work, and sometimes there just isn't any safe place to raise legitimate concerns. It's seems easier just to lower your expectations, make adjustments, go with the flow, and forget that a problem exists. But these problems rarely go away on their own, and the complications they create keep piling up. There's a price to pay for our silence, as Debbie's experience can attest:

My boss is terrible—well, theoretically he does everything "right" according to the management books, but his personality is ... let's just say he can get nasty. Nitpicky. I get very stressed out at work just from dealing with him. Otherwise, I love my job.

Anyway, when he angers me, I sit there and stew, but I don't say anything. Then I spend that entire evening thinking about how I could confront him the following day. I lose sleep thinking about it. The next day comes, and I never say anything. If he acts okay the next day and I feel fine, then I assume I'm over it. Well, that's not actually the case. Without letting it go, you never get over it.

Now I avoid my boss like the plague, but because I work very closely with him and require his input on several of my projects, a lot of my work doesn't get done because I don't want to get in his line of fire. This is making me very unproductive, and I'm not sure what to do. I don't want to bring up things that happened months ago; that would certainly start a screaming session with him. But I may lose my job because I'm not adequately fulfilling my duties. It's hard to get over all the times he's humiliated me and still work productively with him.

Rebuilding the Ladder

Improving relations and communication between management and staff can be the most challenging—and rewarding—process that an individual or a company can undertake. Many of the behaviors, attitudes, and structural problems that define an unhealthy workplace have been institutionalized over many years. It will take time, determination, and courage to turn things around. Fortunately, there are lots of examples of such transformation, and many lessons learned from them. As we saw in the previous chapter, there are plenty of ways for people to facilitate better relations on the job. And while those techniques primarily addressed coworker relations, they also apply to every level of an organization.

> Improving relations and communication between management and staff can be the most challenging—and rewarding—process that an individual or a company can undertake.

Below are two sets of suggestions: an extensive one for managers (since much of the control is in their hands) and a shorter one for those they manage. But don't let the category name stop you from reading both sets. Each side can learn from the other, and indeed that's the only way to build communication bridges that last.

For Managers

• *Remember the "bigger picture."* Managers sometimes assume that their employees don't have a healthy appreciation of the "big picture"—what they and the company are up against and trying to do—but managers need to maintain a larger perspective as well. This perspective includes the importance of good staff relations to achieving the mission of the department and of the entire company. This isn't just about being a good person but about creating the kind of environment where employees are heard and feel trusted to do what they've been hired to do. There are financial bottom lines—if you can't pay the bills, pay your people, and put some money aside to keep the company moving forward, there won't be a company to move—and relationship bottom lines. There's nothing wrong with making money, but how you make it is key. Many companies are financially successful even as they honor their responsibilities to their employees, their communities, and the planet that sustains them. In most cases that is why they are successful. (We will read more about these companies in chapter 8.)

The quality of the relationships you as a manager create with those you manage has a direct influence on how good they feel about their jobs and how easy or difficult it is for you to meet your goals. The amount of energy wasted and time lost dealing with the conflicts and misunderstandings that arise during the normal course of business can be enormous, and many of them are avoidable. This is energy that could be channeled in a much more productive direction. At the same time, expecting your staff to change or your company to change if you aren't willing to as well is unrealistic. Part of your job is acknowledging your own challenges and limitations and deciding how to address them.

• *Walk a mile (or at least a few yards) in their shoes.* Imagine a manager and a staff member sitting across from each other going over the week's schedule. Wouldn't it make a big difference if instead of focusing on the superficial—meetings, deadlines, resources, and so on—they went a step further and addressed the emotional realities that may be involved with that specific job? Can you work with such-and-such a person? What other priorities are you juggling? How have you been feeling about the recent switch in operating systems? are some typical questions that will bring managers closer to the experiences of the people they manage.

When managers seek information from their staff at this deeper level, not so deep that they trespass on private ground but deep enough to show that they care about and maybe even understand their situation, then employees will feel safer about expressing their real needs in getting a job done well. They won't fear that information will be used against them or that admitting their challenges will make them look weak. Open and honest communications (no whining allowed) about our experience at work is a liberating act, both for managers and those they manage. This approach goes beyond the merely functional to empathy and compassion, to a willingness to understand someone's motivations, difficulties, and fears. When everyone in an organization learns to appreciate the challenges of various positions—even those of the janitor, who is burdened by the thoughtlessness of others—then you start to become sensitized to the issues that are important to them. It's another good way to build workplace community and dissolve the barriers that keep us hidden behind positions and titles.

• *Be a role model.* How employees perceive the actions and behaviors of the people who manage them greatly influences how those employees approach their work. Managers have the opportunity to fulfill their roles as mentors and leaders and to set the right tone for a department or a team. If, as a manager, you aren't upholding a higher standard (whether the company is or isn't), don't expect employees to. Don't talk about teamwork and trust, for example, if you tend to isolate yourself and change your story depending on to whom you are talking. Once a manager loses the trust of those he or she manages, it's very difficult to get it back. In the meantime, performance suffers, and everyone looks bad. Instead, set an example for such things as truth telling and compassion; you will inspire the same in those you manage.

Good role models also show good manners; saying "thank you," "please," and so on sincerely reflects a basic respect for another's humanity. Watch for hierarchical language—any words or phrases that reinforce the upper/lower (more/less important) dynamic of the organizational ladder. At Rosenbluth International, a highly regarded travel agency recognized for its emphasis on service, "employees" and "managers" are referred to as "associates" and "leaders." Their value to the company is similarly reflected in the unusual amount of trust, training, and respect they receive. The company's commitment goes well beyond the name changes alone.

All of this doesn't mean that the distinctions between managers and employees should be overlooked—managers do shoulder the weight of greater responsibility—but an effective working team minimizes those differences while emphasizing the value of everyone's input to the success of a project. Managers are leaders by definition; by mirroring the right kinds of behavior, they can create a positive cascading effect throughout their department and the entire organization. People change by being shown, not told. Look at every interaction with employees (or associates) as a chance to lead by example and build stronger working relations. We all need good role models, and we all have the potential to be one.

• *Encourage sincere two-way communication.* Although this tip sounds like a no-brainer, the number of companies and managers that don't encourage quality input from their employees is still a lot higher than it should be. This in spite of the fact that when management and staff take time to share their experiences, trust builds, loyalty grows, and work performance improves. I'm referring to a process of relationship- and knowledge-building in which people come together to create an environment for learning and growth. It's also the best strategy for identifying problems, or potential problems, before they grow into monsters. When people know that honesty is expected and encouraged and won't be punished, they'll be much less inclined to take their grievances or ideas to the water cooler or to simply sit on them until they explode. Such reassurances should come from the top; it's a lot tougher for an employee to go to a supervisor with a problem or an idea then to have a supervisor come to them and ask for input.

Following are some specific ideas for helping managers put their commitment to relationship building into action.

1. **Set aside time for feedback.** Be consistent in providing opportunities for employees to discuss their concerns. These discussions can take place as frequently as every week or every month, or even just twice a year, as long as it's enough to stay connected with your staff and ahead of any problems. Have a loose agenda prepared, so that both you and the employee know what to expect during the meeting. Keep the mood informal; the more comfortable everyone is, the greater the possibility that the feedback will be sincere.

2. **Talk to everyone.** Make sure that all the people you supervise can walk through your open door. Those who don't may be completely at ease with their situations and not feel the need to talk—or they may be so bottled up with frustration that they are afraid to step forward. You'll never know unless you hear it directly from them. And whatever you do, try not to play

favorites. Sure, you may feel more comfortable with some people than with others; that's natural. Just don't let this prevent you from showing equal respect to everyone who reports to you. There will always be something to appreciate about those with whom you have trouble connecting.

3. **Develop cultural sensitivity.** Not all companies have made the shift to preparing for a more diverse workforce, but hopefully that won't keep good managers from learning what they can about the value differences that may exist between cultures. There may also be differences in communication styles, authority relationships, family commitments, and so on. Each group is distinct, and each company will have its own unique situation. One strategy has been to work with an intermediary of your choosing who can comfortably communicate between cultures, acting as a conduit for concerns, ideas, policies, and objectives.

4. **Encourage honesty.** Your words, your body language, and the energy you put out will indicate how receptive you are to hearing the truth about someone's situation. Don't be distracted, and don't be insincere. It's better to do nothing at all than to send a double message that you want to know when you really don't. You too have an obligation to be honest. No matter how "strategic" it may feel to withhold information in certain situations, reconsider your motivations. It's

usually best to keep people in the information loop, out of respect for their need and right to know, as an act of mutual trust, and also to quell rumors, which can quickly have a destabilizing impact on operations.

5. **Establish expectations.** It's important for employees to know what's expected of them, and what they expect of you. This isn't always a comfortable process—both parties can get defensive if they think too much is being asked. But the air will be that much fresher at the end of such an honest exchange. "I need from you...," "I want from you...," and "I hope to get from you..." are all good starting points for sharing and exploration. Experiment with asking employees to set their own goals; this can stimulate creativity and greater ownership of them.

6. **Discuss performance.** Once expectations are clearly understood, the next step is to evaluate if they're being met. Your approach is critical here; to confront with blame or criticism will only spark defensiveness and guilt. Focus instead on how something can be improved. Most employees want to know how well— or even how poorly—they're doing and how they can do things better. There is a popular saying in business: "Praise in public, give feedback in private." I might question the first part—you want to be careful about instigating jealousies—but the second part makes sense. In a safe environment and in a truth-seeking

spirit, almost any issue can be dealt with constructively and compassionately. Good managers are coaches who know how to get the best out of those with whom they work.

7. **Acknowledge good work.** Everyone needs to hear that they are doing a good job. Sometimes it doesn't take much more than a simple, from-the-heart "thank you"—not a generalized thanks for just being in the company, but a pointed effort to show appreciation for a particular success—to lift someone's spirits. It's also important to make sure that the right person (or people) gets the credit.

8. **Solicit ideas and mean it.** The "suggestion box" is frequently used as an example of a company's authentic interest in getting feedback from its employees, but many of these boxes go empty. Or when thoughts or comments do get through, too often they are never acknowledged. Even ideas that end up saving a company money often don't get traced back to the person who came up with them. Make staff input on better ways of doing business a priority, thank the people who go to the trouble to respond, then let them know what, if anything, was done. You don't have to agree with everything that comes in or change a long-standing policy based only on one suggestion, but stay open-minded. And by making an effort to follow-up, even if it's only to explain why an idea won't work,

you will go a long way to fostering better relations. A food co-op I belong to has a big bulletin board with customer requests and complaints tacked all over it on small preformatted memo sheets; every single one of them has a staff response attached. It's remarkably enlightening and makes me believe that the people who run the store really care about what I think.

9. **Deal with issues now.** The path of least resistance is not necessarily the best one to travel when it comes to dealing with problems that come up at work. Some issues—as well as people—do go away over time, but whenever there's trouble under the surface, it's bound to get messy on the surface in the form of interpersonal conflicts, deteriorating performance, higher turnover, and so on. Let's return to Debbie's story of workplace stress. In this case it was she who sat on her problems—to her peril—but the insights she walked away with apply to any problem situation that doesn't get resolved.

> So the lesson I learned is . . . don't keep things bottled up. When you get upset with someone, clear the air. Even if you don't want to confront them, at least offer some bit of communication, like briefly touching upon your feelings. You need to work through barriers with your coworkers—or anyone else for that matter—if you want to sustain a relationship. Communication in which you

feel free to express your thoughts is the key. However, don't rush into conversations, because they may turn out negatively and you'll wind up wishing you hadn't said anything. Think long and hard about what you want the other person to know, and think of his or her feelings and reactions before speaking.

Debbie's experience is another reason why a climate of honesty and safety is so imperative to healthy workplace communication. Good managers accept the reality that some issues—and some emotions—will be difficult and need space and time to sort themselves out. It's probably the most challenging part of any manager's job, but an unavoidable one if a manager is truly committed to breakthrough acts of leadership. Watch for signs of disenchantment; encourage your staff to "get things off their chest." If and when someone does, acknowledge their courage, let them express their pain, ask them what they need to feel better, and then help them to refocus on the future. It's not about being the staff counselor but about helping employees work through their emotions so they can return to their jobs with a renewed sense of purpose.

10. **Be human**. Yes, people in positions of responsibility have a role to fill and certain qualities to project, but that doesn't mean they need to turn into corporate robots or slaves to their egos. Managers can be accessible while maintaining boundaries of authority. In fact,

as a manager, the more vulnerability you show, the more likely the people you manage will trust you and be more forthcoming with their own experiences. This doesn't mean that you have to break down and sob to convince people you're real or to treat everyone like they're your new best friend, but it does mean admitting your mistakes and showing some real feelings: "You know, I really underestimated the time it would take to get those figures together" or "I'm sorry for pairing you up with Martin. I thought the two of you would work well together" are examples of showing one's vulnerability in a professional manner.

Admitting a mistake isn't a sign of weakness; it's an act of courage that employees will respect. It's also an act of trust; you are telling the people you manage that you trust them enough to share an awkward experience, that it's OK not to be perfect, and that we learn from our mistakes only if we look at them honestly. It may take some time for some employees to adjust to working with a more open manager, but as long as your behavior is consistent, they will come to see it as a gift.

The suggestions just presented will make a few corporate executives squirm in their leather chairs. For them, the work world is better off as a simpler place where credibility and competence are measured by military standards of obedience and results; anything else suggests that you're unfit for economic battle. It's an old model that clings tenaciously to the present. But today's business climate demands new abilities, not just technological skills but people skills. There's no substitute for loyalty, and no better way to build it than to treat employees as if your company's life depended on them. It does.

For the Managed

We've seen a few things that managers can do to improve communications with those they manage. Now let's take a brief look at what the "managed" can do to help a supervisor better understand and respond to *their* needs and expectations.

• Keep in mind the pressures that managers are under. You want to make their job easier even as you seek to resolve issues of your own. The better you can understand their goals and how to help meet them, the easier it will be to bring up other issues. This means paying attention, asking questions, and discerning their expectations (to the extent they are discernible—some managers will be hard to figure out). "Ms. Evans, I know how important it is to get this

> There's no substitute for loyalty, and no better way to build it than to treat employees as if your company's life depended on them. It does.

project off the ground soon. What can I do to make it easier?" Find out what information needs they have, such as how frequently they want updates on a project and whether they prefer them in written or verbal form.

• If you're bringing a problem to your manager, be clear about what you need; don't expect him or her to read your thoughts. While something may be obvious to you, it may not be to them. Doing this will require some preparation, some thinking through of what you want to say and why. Look your boss in the eye when you speak, not in a challenging way but to strengthen the contact and to let them know that while you may not be equals in a "corporate" sense, your concerns are real. Start out with a prefacing comment, then transition to the substance of your situation: "Mr. Glenn, I've been working with Todd on this ACME account for several months, now, and it's going pretty well. But something's come up that needs some attention. . . ."

• Pace yourself, keep breathing, and stay in touch with your emotions and how your body feels. These grounding principles will help you stay balanced if you start to lose focus or get nervous.

• Don't manipulate your manager with false expressions of appreciation for his or her work or management style. In other words, don't "brownnose"; in the long term, it's not considered an effective (or a dignified) communication tool. Such partnerships are based on opportunistic loyalties with shallow roots. This doesn't mean that sincere acknowledgments are off-limits; just be careful how and when you use them.

• Admit to your mistakes. A good manager will respect you for it in the same way that you would respect him or her for disclosing a personal screwup. Of course, if you show up every week with a different mistake. . . .

• Complain "diplomatically." Something like, "There's a situation that's been troubling me" will work far better as a lead-in to problem solving than "John's always interrupting me at our weekly meetings." Be firm (but conciliatory) in situations when you feel you're being asked to do too much. "I should finish the Smith project first, otherwise Mr. Gray in accounting will. . . ." is better than "I can't, I'm too busy" or just saying "yes" and then falling asleep at your desk at two on the morning. Recommending a few solutions will always earn big points, even if none of them get used.

• Listen well, don't interrupt, and pause before you reply. This will give you the space to assess what your manager is saying and then to come up with a good response.

• Make sure you get closure if a conclusion needs to be reached; don't let a manager off the hook if you need some kind of answer or some commitment of support. If more time is needed, then agree to a follow-up, or ask them to specify what happens next. Be straightforward. "So, when are you available to meet again? I'll make sure I have those figures and give Erin a call to see what she thinks." Here you've reassured the boss that you'll do what you agreed to do, which is a nice way of affirming the value—and the need—of another meeting.

• Don't let fear stop you from asking for what you need, whether it's resources for a project, feedback on performance, the status of a raise, anything where the road to resolution leads through your boss. You have a right to be told certain things and a right to be heard. Debbie learned the hard way that silence was not an ally. You may not always get what you need, but you'll feel better for having taken the risk, and doing nothing will change nothing. Give yourself permission to step forward with all the power and clarity that you possess.

Frank, the grade school teacher I referrered to at the beginning of the chapter, faced a difficult choice after his principal humiliated him in front of others for trying to resolve an issue that she herself was responsible for. Rather than let it go (though it probably would have come back again, and again), he decided to do something about it:

> I wrote a note to the principal afterward requesting a time when we could meet. When I finally got to speak with her in her office, I closed the door and said we needed privacy. I told her about my feelings, that I was embarrassed about what happened and would appreciate never being yelled at in a public setting again. I suggested that if she was that upset in the future I would prefer that she call me aside and deal with it in private. She denied the actions. I clearly stated the details of the event and assured her that there were many people present and I know that

they all heard the exchange and were just as shocked as I and had indicated it by their expressions. She still said she didn't remember doing it but apologized anyway.

The result didn't bring Frank and his principal any closer, at least not yet, but the confrontation let her know that certain behaviors weren't acceptable. It was also a healing release for Frank, who knew he'd been wronged and had enough self-respect to do something about it and to do so with confidence and integrity.

Always Seek Partnership

As I hope I've made clear, the manager-managed relationship is a complicated one with lots of history behind it, immortalized in countless media images, business case studies, and hard-core experiences. Trust between bosses and employees has been hard to come by, and the challenges to making the relationship work can seem overwhelming. But there is much that can be done—and should be done—because the workplace needs the best efforts of everyone involved to survive.

Some conflict is natural; there are difficult decisions to be made and multiple perspectives to be considered. However, this makes it even more imperative for management and staff to figure out effective ways to address those differences and the legitimate needs behind them. The most successful business partnerships are based on a respectful give-and-take that prioritizes two-way communication; goals can then be set by mutual input that inspires a common effort. When management and staff begin to accept each other as partners and not as adversaries, they will open the door to a new kind of relationship that draws out their strengths rather than buries them. The result is a transformed workplace where everyone has a chance to perform at the peak of their potential.

CHAPTER 6

"It's always a good feeling when a customer asks for you in particular to wait on them."

—STEVE, shoe salesman

"I don't know what your destiny will be, but one thing I do know: the only ones among you who will be really happy are those who have sought and found how to serve."

—ALBERT SCHWEITZER

Treating Customers as Human Beings

When most of us think of customers, we visualize the throngs at a local mall or in line at the grocery store check-out. Or we picture something more abstract, like the sound of a clicking keyboard in the twenty-four-hour world of cyber commerce. We see rows of cubicles filled with people confirming orders, handling complaints, or following up with surveys. But dealing with customers is a fact of life for most of us—the owner of a business supply store, the guy who hooks up your telephone, the hardware vendor for a motorcycle shop, the marketing people in a technology firm, the account rep at an ad agency, the gal at the fast food counter. The citizens of a town are customers of the local police department. Even when I was editor of a small trade magazine I was surrounded by customers. Who were they? The people who read the magazine. My job, and that of everyone else who worked there, was to figure out what these customers wanted and then to deliver it at the highest level of quality we could. Come to think of it, you, the reader of this book, are my customer.

> The long-term success of any business enterprise depends on helping its customers feel good about their experience and the company with which they're doing business.

The long-term success of any business enterprise thus depends on helping its customers feel good about their experience and the company with which they're doing business. This means anticipating and attending to their interests when they're considering a purchase, making sure they're happy with that transaction, and then handling their complaints when they've got a problem (you'll have to take *your* issues up with my publisher...). Communication skills are basic to all three and will often make the difference when someone is deciding whether your company has earned their loyalty. When customers feel as if they've been treated with decency and respect, especially in a world where such expectations have fallen so low, they glow with appreciation. A review of website comments on customer service yielded the following quotes from satisfied patrons:

> I just wanted to let you know that twice I have called your customer help line ... [but] let me preface my comments regarding these calls with an observation of the way customer service (in nearly every industry) has seriously declined. In the past year alone,

I've had issues with television cable service, airlines, computer "superstores," and computer manufacturers, and their customer service was horrible. When I've had occasion to contact your company, however, I have been treated with respect and patience. Both times I was given excellent service—what a refreshing change of pace that was!! I wish I could remember the names of the representatives who helped me, but if there is a way for you to track my calls and give them my compliments, I hope you will, because they certainly deserve to hear them.

Ron is a former building contractor who inspected our home a couple of times during its construction. He found a few things wrong, including one or two which were serious enough to potentially delay our closing. But he approached his job in a non-adversarial manner, understanding that problems are natural and the goal of everybody—him, the building supervisor, the sales agent, my wife and I—was to make sure that we would be happy with our new townhouse. He was very professional, and did not approach it as "I'm going to nail these @#$%&." We were very pleased with the job he did.

Sometimes it takes so little to please someone, and yet at many companies the customer hardly comes first or is only grudgingly put there. Often they're reduced to a unit of revenue or feared as tyrants whose only interest is getting more and more for less and less. The people who deal directly with them can lose interest or become cynical. Even at companies that have made an effort to train their employees to understand the value of good customer relations, there will be days and clients that push our sanity to the limits.

It Starts with Happy Employees

Facilitating good customer relations, like the challenges to harmonizing coworker and staff-management relations, cannot be discussed without at least acknowledging the effects of workplace culture on the motivation of employees to do their best, day after day. If someone feels mistreated or ignored at work, if they don't feel like a valued part of the corporate team, then a "why bother" attitude can easily contaminate their contact with those outside company walls. On the other hand, when employees feel good about themselves at work, they will naturally be inclined to share that contentment, not so much explicitly but in the way they do their jobs. For those in sales and service, such an attitude is infectious and will be felt immediately by customers. Even the most difficult situation can be managed when approached in the right spirit. The moral? Good customer relations begin before you first open your door for business.

Federal Express has a corporate principle that reads, "Customer satisfaction starts with employee satisfaction," and they prove it with such employee-sensitive initiatives as an Open-Door management policy and a Guaranteed Fair Treatment Procedure (see chapter 8 for more about these). Rosenbluth International, the successful and innovative travel agency mentioned in the last chapter, considers happiness a "central strategic objective." CEO Hal Rosen-

> Federal Express has a corporate principle that reads, "Customer satisfaction starts with employee satisfaction."

bluth isn't bashful about linking that commitment to its impact on the people who buy his company's services: "I think that companies today have an obligation to create an environment where people are happy. Because if people aren't happy and they don't like the company they are a part of, if they don't like their leader, then they are really not going to be focusing on the customer. They're going to be focusing on their résumé."

Most companies, however, are run neither by cigar-chomping opportunists nor by cutting-edge innovators. They are well-meaning, overworked collectives trying to keep their customers and clients happy while struggling to adequately train, motivate, and manage a similarly well-meaning and overworked staff. Even as companies spend more and more money finding and preparing good people, the challenges of customer retention and satisfaction remain daunting. Successful customer relations ultimately require systemwide approaches, although it often boils down to each individual interaction between you and the person you're trying to serve.

Relationships That Last

The better companies do know how vital it is to establish long-term relationships with their customers; some of them have even started referring to their customers as partners, associates, or guests, acknowledging this more personal approach. They realize that the foundation of any successful business is made up of the people who come back a second, third, and fourth time. These folks end up spending more money per order than one-time or infrequent shoppers, and they act as goodwill ambassadors for the companies they favor, referring their friends and talking the place up. Frederick Reichheld, a former management consultant for Boston-based Bain & Co., studied the "economics of loyalty" for years and uncovered some startling numbers, some of which were featured in his book *The Loyalty Effect.* Reichheld and Bain found, for example, that:

- repeat grocery store customers spent 20 percent more in months thirty-one to thirty-six than they did during the first six months they shopped there.

- when a credit card company increased its customer retention rate a mere 5 percent, the lifetime value of its average customer increased 75 percent.

- returning customers at a number of popular retail sites spent almost 60 percent more on their visit than first-time shoppers and showed a willingness to extend their buying across multiple product lines.

- U.S. companies lose approximately half their customers in five years.

The challenge, of course, is learning how to turn first-time and occasional shoppers into lifelong friends, which is becoming more difficult every year as competitors sprout like weeds; consumers grow more educated, demanding, and cost-conscious; and discounted prices become the norm rather than the exception. The influences of technology have contributed as well. The Internet, for example, has made store hopping and deal shopping integral to the process of deciding where to spend our money. Loyalties turn into butterflies, flitting from one hopeful site to another. At the same time, the advent of e-mail has brought customers closer to companies in an unprecedented, and sometimes overwhelming, way. According to the Consumer Care Institute, handling the growing volume of e-mail feedback (Did you know there are more than five billion e-mail accounts in the world?) is the number-two challenge in improving customer relations, right behind finding and keeping staff.

To be sure, many companies have responded with renewed efforts to corral the wild consumer. Spending on "Customer Relationship Management" (CRM), a fancy term for software and services that track and record everything there is to know about someone's shopping habits so a company can anticipate their needs, has grown sixfold in the last five years to a billion-dollar-plus industry. Unfortunately, this growing reliance on techno-logical solutions doesn't address the challenges of human-to-human contact. Indeed, despite more options and dropping prices and suitors with sophisticated databases, the American Customer Satisfaction Index (ACSI), pro-duced quarterly by the University of Michigan Business School in conjunction with the American Society for Quality (ASQ) and the CFI Group, fell to its lowest level in the first quarter of 2001 since mid-1999 and overall has been declining steadily across all industries tracked since 1995. Consider this experience of a woman who was hav-ing trouble with her stereo system, posted on a manage-ment consulting website:

> It's two years old, an excellent brand, but intermit-tently works. Fortunately, I had bought an extended warranty. So I take it in for repair. When you walk in, you can feel the bureaucracy, the arrogance, the "we are in control" attitude.
> "How long will it be?" I ask.
> "We don't know."
> "How much will it be?"
> "We don't know."
> Meanwhile, a customer next to me is yelling and screaming after he learns he is not going to get his unit by Christmas as promised. Oh well, kids (and grown-ups) don't need Christmas music—right? Anyway, I have no choice but to leave the stereo. Three weeks later, no action.

"We are still waiting for the parts," they tell me.

One week after that, the store manager fills my ear with how he is being squeezed on the repair reimbursement from my warranty company. By the way, they still don't know how long it will take.

"Have you checked to make sure the part order was correct?" I ask.

"Yes, they are out of stock."

"Can I call them?"

"No."

Two days later: "Sorry, we ordered the wrong part."

The next week I get my beloved stereo back. It works for two days. I unwire it and take it back. A week later I get it back and it still acts up. I give up.

Well, there's a lot going on here, all of it negative and leading to a lost customer. She probably didn't know the first thing about electronic equipment and ended up in the awkward position of dealing with people who couldn't have cared less. She was most likely intimidated, certainly frustrated, and needing some kind of reassurance. The guy yelling next to her didn't help matters and probably made them worse by attacking the salespeople. At several points in this sad scenario the company could have acted very differently and changed that woman's experience:

- By making her feel more welcome when she walked in the door and showing more concern about her problem

- By telling her they would follow up when they got more information
- By following up
- By apologizing for delays
- By offering some compensatory gesture such as an exchange or a loaner or a rebate on another purchase (even if it meant bending the rules a bit)

Sure, we can be awfully fickle buyers, but I do believe that a missing element in the customer relations mix is treating the customer as a human being. I also believe that good communication can help facilitate a more intimate customer experience. It may not guarantee that all the problems of finding and keeping customers will be solved, and some people may not want much more than a "hello" and a "thank you" over the phone, but there's no denying the importance of genuine human contact in an overall customer-centered strategy. It is during your initial contact with customers that they form their first impressions of you and, after a purchase, when they decide if you really do care about their business. Potential "partners" are most vulnerable *and* most cautious when they first consider buying and then when they come to you with a postpurchase problem or question. How they are treated at these critical junctures will make all the difference.

Begin at the Beginning

Reid Systems (a Chicago-based screening tools developer) analyzed thousands of grocery store job applications and, as reported on in *Workforce* magazine (May 2001), made some startling discoveries about the assumptions some people have about the appropriate way to handle customers:

- Forty-five percent of all applicants said they believe that customers should be told when they are wrong.

- Forty-six percent said that customers have to follow the rules if they expect to be helped.

- Thirteen percent said that if customers don't ask for help, it means they don't need it.

- Ten percent said they wouldn't help a customer if her or his request wasn't technically their responsibility.

If you were to create a person who was a composite of all these responses and put him on the shop floor or behind the complaint desk, how do you think he would act? What kind of experience would you, as a customer, have with such a character? Would this salesperson brighten your day, put your needs ahead of everything else? More likely the pressure would be on you to prove you are worthy of his service: "I'm sorry, but you've failed as a customer. Next, please." Sound far-fetched? Maybe, but we've all encountered salespeople whose attitudes stuck to us like soot.

Reid's research shows the obvious importance of hiring and training well and reminds us of the role that corporate culture and values can play in creating an environment that either embraces customers as equal partners or endures them as a necessary evil. In fact, there are many tools available to help a company start prioritizing for the needs of its customers, and several good books devoted exclusively to customer care. Here we'll mostly focus on what you as a self-motivated employee or business owner can do to improve the customer experience, for the customer as well as for you. By "customer experience" I'll refer primarily to situations when there's a problem or a complaint, but much of what follows can apply to any interaction.

A good place to start is to observe if you are approaching your "clients" in the right spirit, if your efforts are focused on making their experience a good one and their lives a little easier. The assumptions you've made about customers and the attitudes that motivate your actions provide that purpose and direction. For example, if your days drag on and every customer starts to look and sound the same, then you no longer see each situation as a unique opportunity to serve or to grow. The job has become an assembly line of recycled complaints from forgettable faces and voices. On the other hand, staff people who see every phone call or every e-mailed feedback form as a chance to build better relations obviously act with a different set of goals in mind.

Embracing the four "intentions" suggested below can make it easier to deal with the challenges of customer service. They may seem simple or self-evident, but it's amazing how distanced actual reality can be from what our minds tell us is so. As a self-assessment exercise, consider for a moment how different—or similar—these four intentions are to the beliefs and attitudes you have right now that influence your dealings with customers. Does the comparison yield any insights? Closing the gaps between what your purpose has become and what it can be will help keep you on the road to customer communication miracles.

The Four Intentions

1. *I will treat my customers as real people.* Yes, they are playing the role of "customer" and you of the "company representative," but beneath these roles are two human beings, each with hopes and fears and quirks and needs, trying to make meaningful contact, even if it's just because a shipment is a few days late. You don't have to ask how their kids are doing or what their weekend was like (then again, in some situations that would be totally appropriate!), but when you treat your customers—even the nasties—with courtesy and respect, you're more likely to get the same in return.

2. *I will find out what my customers need.* That's the obligation you inherit when you are the seller and someone else is the buyer. In fact, the job of anyone who deals with customers is to ensure that people get what they need. This seems obvious, of course, but how many times have you experienced the opposite, when a company or a service rep did all they could to discourage you from getting the result you wanted? How did you feel after that interaction? The

customer may be "wrong" in *how* they present their complaint (they may be angry, demanding, or insulting), but she or he is right in expecting some kind of resolution.

3. *I will satisfy that need.* Try to meet your customer's needs not just because it's your job, but because you really want to help. I can tell immediately if someone is there for me and when they aren't, if they're merely being functional or if they're putting a little extra into their effort. Now some of you may be laboring under difficult conditions. Sweatshop call centers, inferior products, and Swiss-cheese guarantees can make it tough—even impossible—to give customers what they want. And at the end of a long day it's hard to be as fresh as when you started. But unless you've accepted the idea that being of service is a good thing, then customer interactions will as likely sap your energy as reinvigorate it, regardless of the situation. Again, this doesn't mean that you always have to have on your "happy face," but it does imply the need to make service the touchstone commitment you return to every day.

4. *I will do everything I can to inspire my customers to come back.* This is a key intention. It implies that any interaction must be seen as part of a chain of relationship-building opportunities that can add up to long-term loyalty. It also suggests that you don't get many such chances. When you are motivated by this awareness, you won't just dispatch someone's "conflict du jour" but instead give him or her, by way of a positive experience, another reason to return. It's

the difference between apologizing to a stranger you bump into on the street and apologizing to your next-door neighbor in a similar instance. In the second case there's a continuity that needs to be nurtured. Likewise, the sale—or the complaint—is only the beginning.

A footnote: The Reid research study also found that 34 percent of those grocery store job applicants preferred to work behind the scenes rather than directly with customers. Are you in a job that isn't right for you? It's OK if you aren't a "people person," but if that's true and you find yourself in a people-pleasing position, there's bound to be challenges for which you may not be ready. Be honest with yourself, know your limitations, and if working directly with customers isn't your thing, learn what you can from it while finding a position that better suits your skills.

The Problem Is the Solution

About a decade ago, Case Western Reserve University in Ohio conducted what is still considered one of the best studies of its kind on the prevalence of customer dissatisfaction and what was actually done about it. Thousands of households were contacted, and hundreds of people were interviewed. The results confirmed the belief that many people with a complaint about a product or service never take their problem to the offending company or person. In fact, the study found that only 37 percent of those who recalled a dissatisfying experience went back for resolution. The rest of them either kept it to themselves, dumped it on someone else—their friends, their neighbors, their coworkers, even strangers—or got so angry they sought an attorney, filed a report with an agency like the Better Business Bureau, and in general made it their mission to take the company down. This was especially true for a certain group of people who tried for resolution but didn't get it, or didn't get it soon enough.

So widespread is this lack of customer faith in the integrity of corporate America that a website was launched a few years ago called eComplaints.com. This site's purpose is basically threefold: to give consumers a safe place to rant, to give the accused an opportunity to respond, and to reveal to any visitor the results of those exchanges. There are dozens of product categories and literally thousands of complaints to review. Why do people go there?

"Customers report that most vendors make it hard for people to complain," the company literature states. "Corporate websites are rarely set up to allow customers to input specific problem information. Customer-service telephone lines are usually outsourced to call centers, where complaint data are neither collected nor processed in a meaningful way. In many organizations, complaints tend to come in via stray in-trays, with no systematic handling of receipt, response, and analysis. Dissatisfied customers speak of endless phone-hanging, repeated letters, lost time, frustrations. . . . It's easier to change brands."

The lesson here is that complaints are important and should even be solicited; when a company hears from a disgruntled buyer, it should be thankful. The people who are willing to step forward and speak out show that they care enough to do so, while giving the company a chance to make things right and to learn how to do things better in the future. And if service people address those complaints in a spirit of sincere problem solving, using the skills of good communication, they will have taken a giant step closer to making a friend for life.

Listening, compassion, and respect tell the customer that his or her concerns are your concerns. At SAS Institute (which you'll read more about in chapter 8), they call customer interactions "moments of truth," a chance either to "delight" the customer or to ruin his or her perception of the company's commitment to meeting their needs. TMI, a management training and consulting company, has a fully developed, bordering-on-inspirational complaints policy that was turned into a book: *A Complaint Is a Gift: Using Customer Feedback as a Strategic Tool.*

How you handle customers is definitely influenced by your training and your employer's commitment to customer satisfaction, but the intimacy of the moment, when it's only you and the client, is often all that matters. There are choices to be made in that moment that will either affirm the relationship or weaken it; those decisions are up to you.

Communication Tools for Customer Care

Acknowledge their problem. It's important early on to let customers know that they were right in coming forward with their concern. They need to know that you want to know. This is a reassuring gesture that helps to alleviate whatever suspicions they had and gives them confidence that there is a real chance for resolution. "Thank you for letting us know about...," "We appreciate you taking the time to tell us...."

Be polite. Politeness is an underrated skill. We've become so used to informality and even downright insensitivity that we've lost contact with the power of good manners to put others at ease. How many times have you held the door open for someone who simply breezes through without a word of appreciation? Such common courtesies as saying "please" and "thank you" and "I'm sorry," sincerely spoken, can make a surprising difference in the quality of a conversation.

Be patient and listen. Customers will come to you in various states of need and duress. Sometimes they're scared, sometimes they're angry. Their words may timidly stumble out or rain on you like hailstones. Each customer interaction will have its own rhythm and pace. No matter the delivery, it's important to give a customer time to get it all on the table. Take notes if you need to. Listen for content *and* for emotions; both will give you important information. Adapt to the customer's particular style and watch for nuances; he or she may be saying one thing but beneath it wanting something else. Resist the urge to interrupt. If things start to run on a bit, be discerning. When issues start to repeat, gently cut in with something like, "You know, I really understand what you're saying here." This redirects the conversation with a validation—which the customer will appreciate—while creating an opening for shifting toward problem solving. Don't put him or her on the defensive with an, "OK, I heard you the second time" kind of comment. Remember, this is the customer's time, not yours.

Restate for accuracy. Restating your customer's words is an exercise in seeking clarity and a common tool of those in mediation and facilitation professions. After a customer is done speaking, you repeat what you thought you heard. This ensures not only that you got it right but also that she has said what she wanted to say. "I want my money back." "So, you want a refund on your purchase?" That's an easy one, but it can get more complicated if a tumble of issues is coming at you or someone isn't clear about what he wants. "So, what you're saying is…" or "Let me repeat that to be sure I heard you right" are two approaches for getting both of you on the same page.

Let 'em steam. A lot of customers who come to you with a problem will be angry. These are the ones who feel they've been misled or disrespected or have had this problem before or who keep getting shuttled from one intimidated agent to another. The best thing to do here is to let them have their say. An occasional word of support—a "yes" or an "of course" or a "sure"—gives them permission to keep unloading. This is OK, because until they get it all out they won't have much room for anything constructive. Your challenge is to stay with them through this process and not take it personally if they start pointing a finger at you and not the company. Be firm if you need to—"Thank you, I really hear what you're saying. Now let's see what we can do about it"—but don't fight with them. Many will want to bait you, draw you into the ring: "Are you guys always this lame?" Don't go there. Try responding with something like, "I know this has been tough for you, but I'm here to help fix it." Or put the question to them: "What would help you feel satisfied here?" Respect their need to work through their frustrations, keep nudging the process toward resolution, and you'll likely end up with a willing partner in problem solving.

Stay detached. When strong emotions come your way, don't take them on. As noted above, you will often be a target of customer discontent. Many customers may personalize their anger by holding you responsible, and sometimes it's hard simply to ignore the power of such fury. Just remember: The emotion is theirs, not yours. You are there to help, as soon as they give you a chance. An image I like to use is that of a pane of glass. Let the strong emotions of others pass through you like light (even dark light) passes though a window. At the same time, be careful about oversympathizing. Some empathy is absolutely necessary, but if you perpetuate a victim mentality, it will take that much longer to come to a resolution.

Stay centered. A lot comes at you when you're dealing with customers, and some of it can be difficult to take. If they're angry, for example, you are the only visible target for their discontent. To avoid letting their drama become your drama, it's important to stay in control of your own emotions. Breathing steadily, dropping your shoulders, inhaling and exhaling deeply, taking short contemplative breaks (someplace quiet), even smiling (yes, I've tried it—over the phone—and it works!) are some simple things you can do to keep from getting caught up in the negativity of customer complaints. Inner calm will also help you be a better communicator.

Take responsibility. The buck has to stop somewhere, and the last thing a customer wants to feel is that she's being "jerked around." This means that you'll see her problem to the end, even if it means talking with a supervisor, calling the customer back, or filling out a special report—whatever it takes. To state unequivocally, "I'll take care of this, Mrs. _____, and then call you as soon as I get the information," and then following through, is a surefire way to start rebuilding any bonds of trust that may have been broken. It also means that if someone's issue is "not in your area," you'll make sure it gets to the appropriate place. I've had service people stay with me on the phone until someone else actually was waiting for me on another line. I've also been routed into a black hole. Which would you prefer?

Choose your words carefully. Choosing our words is the most subtle challenge of all and one that has been discussed several times already in this book. Simply stated, what we say and how we say it can open doors or close them. It's no different with customers than it is with coworkers or managers. In the case of customers, especially disgruntled ones, the challenge is to validate their concerns, keep things positive, avoid placing blame, and keep the conversation moving toward a successful conclusion. If, for example, a customer comes to you with a question that has an obvious answer ("How do I turn on my computer?"), a "Didn't you see the button?" response won't be nearly as effective as "There's a small silver button on the upper right-hand side." If you don't have an immediate solution or if your options are limited, find a way of saying so that either gives you more time or puts the situation in a better light: "I'll talk to my supervisor" or "There are a couple of things we can try."

Problem solve by having options ready. The purpose of customer contact is to give customers what they want, whether it's a different pair of shoes or an upgraded guarantee or another copy of a bill or money back on a shoddy product. The entire conversation should be directed to that end: hearing them out, getting the necessary information, keeping emotions from escalating, and then reaching a satisfying conclusion. Know what's in your power to control, and know where to go when there's something you can't resolve. A long "umm" in answer to a question isn't a good strategy for gaining a customer's confidence.

> What we say and how we say it can open doors or close them.

Follow up. Following up may not be the front-line service agent's or salesperson's responsibility, but it's a vital step in the chain of successful customer service. Most customer follow-ups are made for one or two reasons: when someone at a company has agreed to do something for you and then promises to let you know what happened, or when he or she is inquiring whether a recent transaction you had with the company was satisfactory. There seems to be an increase in this second type of follow-up; it suggests a more savvy approach to improving customer relations. According to Tom Terez's Workplace 2000 Employees Insight Survey (the basis for his book *22 Keys to Creating a Meaningful Workplace*), nearly eight out of ten of those surveyed had access to some form of customer input and feedback, including survey data, focus groups, individual interviews, letters, and call transcripts. As long as the real purpose isn't to sell more products, the chance to offer feedback, positive as well as negative, should be embraced by customers.

We're All Human

I want to stress again how meaningful I think it is to treat your customers as real people whose needs are important to you. Most of us can tell when someone cares about our situation. You hear it in his voice, you sense it in his patience, you feel it in his willingness to go the distance. We're all desperate to experience real human contact, to hear a kind word or to offer one in return. The world is so filled with superficial interactions that even the smallest gesture can have an impact. Satisfied customers are the vital link to a company's success. It's not a numbers game, it's a people game, if it's a game at all. If you take care of your customers, they'll take care of you. Communicate openly and honestly and with an intent to serve, and they'll stay with you in good times and bad.

CHAPTER 7

"Just because we increase the speed of information doesn't mean we can increase the speed of decisions. Pondering, reflecting, and ruminating are undervalued skills in our culture.

—DALE DAUTEN,
syndicated business
columnist

"Democracy is based upon the conviction that there are extraordinary possibilities in ordinary people."

—HARRY EMERSON FOSDICK,
early 20th-century
preacher/orator

Working in Groups

ew pronouncements in business strike as much fear into people's hearts as "Let's schedule a meeting." At least one study has shown that there is a direct correlation between time spent each week in meetings and an employee's desire to find another job. And let's face it: Most meetings take a supreme human effort to get through unscathed. Unfocused, too long, poorly planned, indecisive—meetings in America, and probably many other places in the global corporate world, rank just below weekend overtime as a favored workplace activity. The problem is, we can't get along without them—at least a few of them—so it makes sense to figure out just what it will take to make them work better.

There are many kinds of meetings, of course, from the ones measured in minutes that go on every day, to more substantive gatherings that can last a few hours, to all-day seminars, weekend workshops, and staff retreats. In fact, team building and collaborative decision making are becoming the norm in an economy that is moving away from traditional top-down management models. More and more employees

> More and more employees are being called forth to participate as equals in interactive groups that have the authority to make decisions and carry them out.

are being called forth to participate as equals in interactive groups that have the authority to make decisions and carry them out. This is a positive change that can empower any member of an organization to feel like a valued part of the company's continued success. Leadership skills are unearthed as everyone gets a chance to put forward ideas and work with others toward a common goal. The chance to interact more intimately with fellow workers can break down the walls that separate us; in this case, familiarity breeds not contempt but appreciation of our differences and respect for what each person has to offer. Effective group process can be a powerful tool for enlightened decision making and action.

That being said, the ideal and the reality are often at odds. As we've seen in earlier chapters, there are multiple potholes on the road to workplace harmony, and when all those potted roads intersect in the same room, traffic jams and chaos can occur. Though we may have the best of intentions, many of us simply don't have the skills or the experience to interact effectively with our peers in a group setting. More important, if meetings or group work are vaguely planned or poorly designed, if agendas are unclear or unrealistic, if there's no trust or leadership in the room, then there's little chance that people will be empowered to work together productively.

In this chapter we'll focus on meetings that are substantive enough to involve a group of people and take several hours to several days; the basic dynamics will be essentially the same for all of them. As for shorter meetings of the "touch-base" variety that usually last less than an hour and sometimes for just a few minutes, the suggestions in chapter 4 that address coworker relations are the best place to start honing those skills, with a few minor additions:

- Make sure you agree on how much time to allot to the meeting. Even short meetings can run on if there isn't respect for the clock. "How long do we want to do this?" or "How much time should this take?" or even "How much time do you have to spare?" will lead to a realistic sense of when you'll want to be finished.

- Be prepared. Meetings go much quicker if you have everything you need to make necessary decisions.

- Take notes. A lot can be said in a short period of time, and while we think we'll remember everything, inevitably we'll forget the very idea that needed our specific follow-up. Notes also act as an effective paper trail of issues raised and decisions made.

- Decide what, if anything, needs to be done next and who will do it.

- Decide when, or if, there needs to be another meeting, and if there does, write yourself a note (or use some other reminder, short of a permanent tattoo).

Most of these kinds of meetings are both informal and functional, and that's as it should be. By following a few simple rules and approaching them as you would any opportunity to work well with another, you can help integrate them seamlessly into your other activities.

As for those meetings at which more is at stake, their success will depend on the impacts of three areas:

1. Management support and the corporate culture, which can include departmental traditions and the tone set by certain authority figures.

2. The purpose of a meeting and how well it has been planned.

3. The meeting itself, which includes the physical setup, how well its purpose and goals are communicated to attendees, the atmosphere of participation that's created, and the actual process of working together.

Excutive Support

The influence of corporate culture on a company's climate of trust and the quality of communications between and among employees and customers has been a drumbeat theme throughout this book. The role that company culture plays in providing (or depleting) the energy needed to do the best job possible cannot be stressed enough. Similarly, when it comes to group situations such as meetings, a company's track record in planning them, supporting them, and following through on what happens next can make all the difference in how we approach them and what we expect. How many meetings have you walked out of thinking "same ol', same ol'" or "business as usual"? And it's not just staff people who may feel the drag; managers can be just as indifferent if they haven't "bought in" to a meeting's objective or feel they have more to lose than to gain. Such lack of enthusiasm among managers will often rub off on staff: "Well, if they aren't interested, why should we be?"

In extreme cases, some companies and managers assign a mollifying purpose to meetings, thinking that anything said at all is better than nothing. The birthplace of cynicism (and rumor and distrust) is a company's belief that it can ignore or manipulate the informational needs of its employees and their desire to participate in true decision making. A management consultant on the East Coast with a client list of the most successful blue-chip companies in the world told me of an instance when the minutes of a closed-door meeting that were to be circulated among staff were substantially doctored before they were released. This is clearly the sign of a dysfunctional work culture (in spite of its economic success), but also a gross example of how the efforts of any

> Well-planned and well-executed meetings are wonderful opportunities to create company-wide buy-ins and a sense of communal well-being.

group will not bear fruit unless a company's leaders support the process and respect the outcomes.

In most cases, however, there's a legitimate interest in using such meetings productively, whether they address proposed changes in company policy or tackle such challenges as strategic planning or developing mission statements. Well-planned and well-executed meetings, approached in a spirit of teamwork and problem solving, are wonderful opportunities to create company-wide buy-ins and a sense of communal well-being. They are also excellent vehicles for addressing important issues and moving through them with sometimes surprising speed.

Depending on the significance of a particular meeting, management and staff can help ratchet up enthusiasm levels by communicating in several ways:

• An authority figure can step forward and endorse its value. This endorsement could take the form of an e-mail to all participants, encouragement during a premeeting meeting (a short one, of course), through a company newsletter, and so forth.

• Affected managers can speak individually to staff, send their own e-mail endorsements, post information on a bulletin board, or address a larger group at a regularly scheduled meeting.

• Staff can ask questions about its intent and hoped-for outcomes: "What does the company want to achieve here?" "What will it expect from me?" "How will it affect what I do?" "How will it affect what others do?" Some of the answers will depend on the meeting itself, but raising the issues in advance will make it seem more real and immediate.

Time is precious, and people are busy. If they can make the connection between a meeting's value and their on on-the-job experience, they will be that much more willing to give it their best. Management's responsibility is to bring that enthusiasm to the surface.

Why Meet?

There are countless reasons for having a meeting, and in some situations few communications skills are needed other than the ability not to fall asleep (nonverbal communication!), for example, when the director or president calls the troops together for a report on next year's budget. As the meetings and groups become more complicated and interactive, though, different skills are needed. Some of them will be useful regardless of the circumstances; patience, active listening, respect, and so on are universal connectors. Still, working in a group is different from working one-on-one, and so too the strategies for participating and being heard will differ.

Most groups come together in three situations:

1. When information is presented. Here I'm referring to one-way communications, such as when an authority figure or a designated representative faces a room full of people and makes a presentation. It could be about anything—a new contract, a new policy, impending layoffs, and so on. Whatever the content, the primary purpose is to deliver information about a decision that has already been made. The job of those in the audience is to listen—carefully, if possible—and then to ask clarifying questions if prompted.

2. When discussion is encouraged or information exchanged. These gatherings are more informal and can involve anything from feedback sessions between staff and management to brainstorming sessions about specific topics or assessing a group's feelings about an issue that's come up. At such meetings no decisions are made, but the best of them are excellent forums for tapping into the collective wisdom of participants.

3. When decisions need to be made. These meetings, which can be one time only or ongoing, have the distinct purpose of coming to a conclusion—a recommendation or a statement of action—about how to handle a particular issue. Decision making models include everything from majority rules (the U.S.

political system) to full consensus, with a few variations in between.

The planning process for the first type of meeting is usually straightforward; they are announced by a memo or e-mail or emerge impromptu when important news suddenly comes up. The other two types rely on good planning to be effective. This means that their purpose is clear, the right people have been selected to attend, a structure for getting input has been put together, and preferred outcomes have been defined. This can be a complicated process, but it's vital to the success of any group effort, and breakdowns at any point can sabotage the entire operation. The job of the group leader, department head, or project facilitator is to ride herd on this process, which requires input from many people. Once an appropriate program is finalized, the stage is set for what comes next.

Maximizing Group Process

In the same way that good customer relations start before the first customer walks through the door, effective group process starts before anyone walks into a room—with a well-thought-out game plan, the support of upper management, and a physical environment conducive to clear thinking. A morning session in an appropriately sized, well-lit room with comfortable chairs that are placed so everyone can see each other is ideal.

As a participant, you'll probably know in a general way why you're there—to brainstorm about a particular policy or to decide on a mission for the new department—but you still need a bit more preparation before the process actually begins. A big part of this preparation is knowing what's expected of you and the group. Much will revolve around the agenda, which includes all the items to be discussed, in what order, and for how long. In many cases—especially in the case of all-day affairs or weekend retreats—the agenda is created by the group itself or at least revised based on group input. A group leader or facilitator usually manages this process, but it's best if everyone is involved. In fact, while there may be a designated someone whose job it is to keep things moving and all participants engaged, a group will not succeed unless each participant plays an active role. In some situations, such as brainstorming sessions or short, relatively unstructured meetings, there may not be a "leader" or an agenda, but some kind of structure will need to be established (for example, basic objectives, time limits) before the meeting actually starts.

When the room is set, everyone's in place, the agenda (if needed) is clear, and the goals are understood, it's time to begin the dialogue. I use the word *dialogue* because I think it best describes the essence of what happens—or could happen—next. The great physicist and philosopher David Bohm, whom I discovered spent many of his later years exploring the nature of communication and collective thinking (he wrote *On Dialogue* in 1996, shortly before his death), once described the word as suggesting "meaning flowing through"—the natural outcome when a group of people working together acts out of trust in pursuit of higher truths. The word *dialogue* suggests exploration and learning, a result yet to be known. It can happen between two people or among as many as can comfortably fit into a large room—even an auditorium. It happens when group members have suspended their attachment to a single right answer and opened up to other possibilities. Significantly, these possibilities can only be discovered when every participant is fully involved.

Many of the groups with which I've worked rely on a set of "operating principles" or "ground rules" to suggest what is and isn't appropriate behavior. These represent the rules of engagement, shared guidelines that are explicitly agreed on by the group before the process begins. They aren't designed to be parental; rather, they help each person manage him- or herself and engage with the group in a way that is comfortable, safe, and productive. They are designed to prevent abusive conduct and minimize—but not eliminate—conflict, for there is always room for respectful dissent if it ultimately leads to a deeper understanding of the issues. This is also the time when the rules of decision making are made. Is consensus required on every decision, or

> The word *dialogue* suggests exploration and learning, a result yet to be known.

will the group accept less than complete agreement?

The sum total of these considerations creates the blueprint for participating in a group process. Essentially they *are* the process. In fact, the way that people share ideas, listen to one another, and make decisions in a group is often as important as, and sometimes more important than, the actual outcomes. You will work with these people again, and who doesn't want to walk out of such a gathering feeling good about what happened and about *how* it happened.

The most common of these guiding principles are discussed in more detail below. They aren't appropriate to every situation in which a group of people come together to discuss specific issues and/or make decisions, but they are common enough—and important enough—to apply to many of them.

Operating Principles for Group Interaction

Treat everyone with respect. The foundation of successful group communication is accepting that everyone in the room has legitimate interests, concerns, and ideas and a right to share them. And while the new hire in accounting may be shoulder to shoulder with the department head, all are considered equals in such a process.

Keep an open mind. Try to start any group process from scratch; in other words, don't walk in with preconceived notions of a best outcome. While it's tough to ignore your own beliefs and opinions, there is always something to be learned from other points of view: new information, a twist you hadn't thought of, potential solutions revised and improved. This doesn't mean that you should diminish your ideas—they are as valuable as anyone else's—just that you be as open to the suggestions of others as you'd want them to be to yours. Also, be tolerant of ambiguity as clarity forms around various issues. This "don't know, not there yet" space is a healthy part of the process, allowing for a full range of input and evaluation.

Actively listen. When others are speaking, your job is to make sure you understand what they're saying. Don't interrupt, but when they're done feel free to ask clarifying questions such as, "Are you saying that...?" or "Do you mean...?" or "Can you repeat...?" At times you'll be compelled to react midstream, but resist until there's a proper opening. The most egregious case of nonlistening I've experienced was at a local community meeting where planning recommendations were being developed for the county. One impassioned woman just couldn't keep quiet; whenever another's point of view conflicted with her own, she'd burst into vocal defense. This was obviously a problem for the group, but also a problem for her. Whether or not her ideas had merit became less of an issue than the fact that she wasn't respecting the process.

Share openly and honestly. Each participant agrees to be honest and forthcoming with others in the group and that the spirit of the conversations should be constructive. The goal is to build a knowledge base that will lead to understanding and/or enlightened decision making. Such things as hidden agendas, "political posturing," or withholding a concern because you aren't sure it's legitimate distort the process of full and frank disclosure. It is important to be discerning, and certain issues are more sensitive than others, but the best outcomes for all involved depend on each person's willingness to not hold back.

Make it safe for others. Open dialogue can only happen when people feel safe; otherwise the process will never move beyond superficial discussions. The group thus acknowledges everyone's vulnerability and explicitly states that there will be no personal attacks. In some situations confidentiality may be an issue and the group will agree that nothing said can ever be used later against a particular individual. In short, each person must risk trusting both one another and the process. This may not happen right away; unless there's been a history of strong and effective communication among the people involved, the atmosphere is likely to start out a little tense. But as trust and openness build in a group, even "undiscussables" can be slowly drawn out and worked with. A statement such as, "I realize this is a sensitive issue, but in order to move forward with this discussion I think we should talk about. . ." will test the group's willingness to go deeper.

Don't be afraid to contribute. A successful group process depends on everyone's perspective being shared. There will naturally be people who are more vocal than others, more comfortable in groups, or more knowledgeable about a particular subject, and

> A successful group process depends on everyone's perspective being shared.

it's fine if they end up with more floor time. You don't have to be like them, but it is important that you too speak your mind. Some of the quietest people I know surprise themselves by saying the wisest things.

Agree to disagree. The point of working with others in pursuit of a common goal is to encourage open discussion of ideas. Needless to say, things won't always go smoothly, and inevitably there will be disagreement. That's OK, because it often takes time and some spirited debate to ferret out the best insights and information. Fortunately, such give-and-take rarely gets out of hand, because the "rules of engagement" have created a container that can control the heat. "Clarifying" is done respectfully; one disagrees with the idea and not the person, and everyone in the room gets a chance to weigh in and evaluate each point of view. If the purpose of the meeting is primarily informational, then it's relatively easy to move on. When decision making pressures are present and important disagreements remain, then other strategies are needed (see below).

Take mutual responsibility. This ground rule asks participants to be aware of both their own needs as well as the needs of everyone else in the group. A nice way to think of it is to be "other-oriented." Basically, if you're happy with an outcome and someone else isn't, then the solution is only partially successful. For example, if you know that Bill is really uncomfortable but isn't saying anything (he's not being responsible for himself), you can step up and try to find a way to bring him into it. A subtle approach—"I'd like to hear what others think"—can sometimes open a door, but if you think being direct is better, then say something that doesn't put Bill on the defensive: "Bill, what do you think?" or "Is this OK with you, Bill?" are better than, "Bill, you don't like this solution, do you?" It's kind of a "foxhole" principle: We're all in this thing together, and we're all getting out alive.

Monitor yourself. This rule asks participants to observe their own behavior and be sure that it's consistent with the goals of the group. It means, among other things, not talking too long or too loud or too frequently; not repeating what's already been said; listening when others are speaking; asking questions if something is unclear; not being afraid to express discomfort but being willing to explain your feelings; feeling free to criticize an idea as long as you don't make it personal and it has a constructive element; keeping your comments pertinent to the conversation; and so on.

Lighten up! A humorous touch never hurts; in fact, it usually helps.

A Word About Decision Making

Certain communication issues are specific to the way a group makes, or is directed to make, decisions. Majority-vote situations are the most straightforward; after the point of a discussion has been thoroughly explored, someone, usually a designated leader, calls for a vote. The numbers are tallied, and the choice with the most votes wins. All group interaction occurs before the vote; after the vote the group moves on. The same is true of decision making models that use two-thirds and three-quarters majority voting procedures. In these cases, though, the effort to find unity in the group will increase, because the level of agreement required to make a decision is higher than it is with simple majorities.

The goal of consensus, on the other hand, is to reach an agreement that everyone can accept, even if they may not like it. ("Unanimity," on the other hand, is when everyone likes a solution equally well and has an equal commitment to it.) In consensus-seeking situations, almost always guided by a skilled facilitator or group leader, there is greater pressure on a group's ability to work together and thus on the quality of communication within it. Since groupwide agreement is needed, the process leading up to that point asks participants to be especially committed to finding common ground while honoring wholeheartedly the guidelines of dialogue mentioned above.

On the upside, it means that a broader range of options is considered, that all minority views are given fair hearing, and that solutions will be offered that meet the major concerns of all involved. On the downside, it's invariably a longer process than other models, such as voting; it relies more on people respecting opposing views; and it strongly emphasizes the ability of participants to be patient, clear thinking, and clear speaking. Resolving disagreements successfully is especially important. If agreement isn't reached, the group has several options, among them, addressing the dissenter's concerns and revisiting the original solution; recording the dissenting disagreement but asking the individual or subgroup to allow the majority view; preparing a minority report and letting another authority decide.

Other Things to Watch For

The ground rules above are excellent tools for guiding behavior in group situations. Nevertheless, working closely with people we may not know or may not like can pose communication challenges that require an extra bit of effort and vigilance to overcome. A few of them are listed below.

"He's still my boss." Most group processes benefit by an egalitarian spirit where there is no hierarchy, but if your boss or some other authority figure is sitting across from you, it's

difficult to be totally honest no matter how earnestly you're told it's safe. You may feel intimidated and self-conscious; past experiences may make you wary. The best way to confront this situation is to admit it to the group, not defensively but as a matter of information sharing: "You know, I still feel a little uncomfortable talking about _____ with Mr. Ross over there." This takes the secrecy out of the issue, lets people know what you're really feeling, gives others a chance to support you, and gives Mr. Ross a chance to reassure you in front of the entire group.

"Am I part of the solution?" This is a reminder of the importance of self-awareness—watching what we say and how we say it and the influence our words have on the group and its goals. Some of these issues relate to general communication techniques that we've explored in earlier chapters, but many have to do with the specific effect of specific comments and actions. When you speak, for example, do you find yourself always focusing on the same person, such as a friend or the group leader, and not on the group itself? Do you try to align with others or form decision-influencing cliques? Do your comments tend to build on another's input or compete with or criticize what's just been said? Do your ideas tend to be specific ("We should have a two-hour training session every month") or more general ("We need more training")?

In *The Skilled Facilitator,* Roger Schwartz characterizes participant behavior as basically one of three types: functional (enhancing a group's effectiveness by providing clarifying information); dysfunctional (reducing a group's effectiveness by disrespecting others, arriving late, and so on); and counteractive (returning a group to effectiveness by addressing the negative influences of others). Schwartz says that the success of most groups depends on how much counteractive behavior exists because of all the dysfunctional interactions that can go on. Can we be self-aware enough to know which type of behavior we're in at any point during a group process?

What if someone criticizes my idea? The answer to this one (at least in theory) is easy: Don't take it personally. At the same time, don't be afraid to defend yourself. Well-thought-out reasons and logical conclusions, however, will be much more effective than defensive or counterattacking maneuvers. Strong emotions may sway some people, but generally they'll be a distraction if you're trying to convince a particular individual or the entire group that you have a good suggestion. If the person criticizing your idea isn't someone you particularly like, then more complicated feelings will arise. Either way, keep your cool, stick to issues and not to personalities, and be open to the possibility that you may not have the better mousetrap.

Nonverbal neon. Research has shown that more information is conveyed nonverbally through our body language than it is verbally. Think of a flirtation across a room or an angry little boy or someone haggling at a flea market and the variety of nonverbal messages being sent by the people involved. It's no different where we work; we're giving off all kinds of signals all hours of the day. Most of the time what your body is saying doesn't matter, because everyone's doing their thing and there isn't the time or interest to pay much attention. But when you're communicating one-on-one body language starts to count, and in a room full of people those signs become amplified. As a matter

> As a matter of communication integrity and out of respect for others in the group, be aware of what you're saying when you aren't speaking.

of communication integrity and out of respect for others in the group, be aware of what you're saying when you aren't speaking. The more attentive you look when someone is trying to explain a difficult point, for example, the more comfortable she'll feel and the more likely she'll say what she needs to say—and what you probably need to hear.

Real Meetings, Real Work

Working with colleagues in a group situation can be a great way to get things done and to break new ground. The challenges are different from those you encounter when you're dealing with issues in more intimate settings such as with a coworker or a boss, but the communication skills you practice with them come in handy in a group as well. Don't dismiss meetings with such brush-offs as "I have real work to do." Good work can and does get accomplished when people come together in the right spirit to achieve a common goal. And the relationships you can form as a result of that process can carry over into the day to day, enhancing that sometimes elusive sense of community that makes work a more satisfying experience.

CHAPTER 8

"When we talk about quality, we are talking about the quality of product and service. But we are also talking about the quality of our relationships and the quality of our communications and the quality of our promises to each other. And so, it is reasonable to think about quality in terms of truth and integrity."

—MAX DEPREE, Herman Miller CEO

"The primary purpose of a company is to serve as an arena for the personal development of those working in the company. The production of goods and services and the making of profits are by-products."

—ROLF OSTERBERG, Swedish business philosopher

What the Best Companies Are Doing

W e've talked a lot about building better relationships with the people you work with and the many challenges that can make the process so difficult. I have made frequent references to the enormous influence that workplace culture has on the willingness, and even the ability, of employees to step out of their stereotypical roles. In chapter 1, I introduced the Great Place to Work® Institute and its commitment to finding companies that put the needs and interests of their employees first. There's also the Malcolm Baldrige National Quality Awards, given to companies that have shown significant improvement in seven different areas, and *Business Ethics* magazine's "100 Best Corporate Citizens," which recognizes companies based on their financial performance *and* their commitment to multiple stakeholder groups (including community and environment).

All the companies honored by these awards have the same competitive pressures as any other business, the same hiring challenges, the same need to watch the bottom line while tending to the interests of their various constituents. But they

> Quite a few companies are making a positive difference in the lives of the people who work for them by tearing down the walls that have separated functions and positions and departments and constituencies.

seem to do most of these things better than anyone else, *and* they're financially successful. In fact, quite a few companies, both large and small, are making a positive difference in the lives of the people who work for them and the people they serve by tearing down the walls that have separated functions and positions and departments and groups. They still struggle like other companies, ride the economic waves up and down, stumble through unexpected crises and unfortunate mistakes, but through it all they are able to keep the integrity of their commitments intact—in other words, they may bend, but they don't break. They serve as role models for any organization that wants to transform its staff and its workplace into an enduring force for change by making communication, relationship, and authentic community building central to its mission.

Below is a small sampling of those companies and their people-driven policies. Most have received awards for their achievements, and some are only known by word of mouth. All of them have expanded their mission beyond business-as-usual. The first three responded to a series of specific questions asking them to describe just what it is that makes their company special. I follow those with a few brief snapshots of other companies that stand out from the crowd.

SAS Institute

This company, based in Cary, North Carolina, specializes in "business intelligence" software and services. It has enjoyed double-digit sales growth for each of the past twenty-four years and boasts a client list that includes 90 percent of all Fortune 500 companies and customers in 111 countries. SAS was voted number three in *Fortune* magazine's most recent list of "100 Best Companies to Work For," has been in the Top 10 for each of the five years that the list has been compiled, is a twelve-year honoree on *Working Mother* magazine's "100 Best Companies for Working Mothers," and has garnered numerous awards for its technology products.

At the heart of the SAS business model is this motto: "Satisfied employees create satisfied customers.... If you treat employees as if they make a difference to the company, they will make a difference to the company." This philosophy has "never wavered," says company spokesperson Kim Darnofall, not since co-founder, CEO, and president Jim Goodnight first committed to making SAS a workplace where employees would want to be.

SAS broke the mold for how businesses treat employees. In 1981, one year after the company moved to its current world headquarters, SAS became a pioneer in corporate childcare by providing onsite day care for children of employees. In the same year, the first cafeteria providing high-quality, company-subsidized food opened. An onsite health-care center that employs two physicians and a group of family nurse practitioners and a recreation and fitness center are further signs of a company committed to the well-being of its employees and their family members. And those employees are committed to SAS. The company's turnover rate is consistently less than 5 percent in an industry where the average rate is closer to 20 percent. This continuity creates an environment where friendships and collegial working relationships can thrive.

The company doesn't shy away from internal challenges and has successfully integrated cutting-edge technology in dealing with them. Darnofall recalls,

> When a representative sample of our employees was surveyed for last year's *Fortune* application, one of the most common complaints was that they didn't always have a clear understanding of the executive's vision for the company's future. In response, our company president committed to hosting "Quarterly Updates" via an in-house webcast. Everyone at the company can tune in live and watch it from their office. Some departments gather in conference rooms to watch. Employees can even submit questions online—anonymously if they prefer—during the presentation. They are addressed at the end of

the talk. Within several hours of the event, a recap is written and an archived version is posted on the company intranet, enabling people all around the world to watch at their convenience.

The company regularly conducts employee satisfaction and management-feedback surveys. These are done via the Web and are anonymous. Results are published. In the case of the management-feedback surveys, managers receive their own results, and those results are shared with their manager as well. Managers are then encouraged to discuss survey results with their direct reports.

Policies and training programs designed to facilitate open, honest, and effective communication between and among staff and stakeholders are handled by the Professional Education and Development department. It's the philosophy of PED, says Darnofall, that "learning should be fun." The group offers an extensive array of classes, such as interpersonal communication, active listening, PowerTalk, and dealing with difficult people, where employees throughout the company have the opportunity to learn together. The PED staff also customizes activities and curricula to meet the needs of a specific department or division. In both general and customized training events, employees experience extensive opportunities for personal and professional growth.

SAS also has an "open-door" policy—literally and figuratively—regarding communications. Office doors remain open. Every employee has his or her phone extension and e-mail address published on the company intranet. People can (and do, reports Darnofall) send e-mail directly to the company president. "He's often seen in the cafeteria, where employees are free to approach him," says Darnofall. "He goes through the line like everyone else," At SAS, if you look around one of the three cafeterias at lunch or watch an aerobics class in the new fitness center, you're likely to see executives mingling comfortably with other employees.

Southwest Airlines

Southwest has long been considered one of America's stand-out airline companies, and while the entire industry struggled following the September 2001 terrorist attacks, the company continued to draw praise for its forward-thinking policies and motivated workforce. It boasts the industry's highest cumulative customer satisfaction record and won an unprecedented five consecutive "Triple Crowns"—best on-time record, best baggage handling, and fewest customer complaints—in the mid-1990s. Southwest was the first airline to offer a frequent flyer program based on trips taken and not number of miles flown, while pioneering senior discounts, Fun Fares, Fun Packs, and ticketless travel, among other unique programs.

Like other progressive and successful companies, Southwest is a people-oriented culture that puts a high value on the needs of its employees. Public relations director Linda

Rutherford describes what draws people to Southwest and keeps them there.

> The corporate culture at Southwest is based on a family or community-oriented feeling. In the hiring process, we look for people who are altruistic, who have a teamwork spirit and a sense of humor. Our culture is one that encourages people to have fun and work hard, and as for values, Southwest employees follow the golden rule. The mission of the company is dedication to the highest quality of Customer Service delivered with a sense of warmth, friendliness, individual pride, and Company Spirit. We also provide our employees a stable work environment with equal opportunity for learning and personal growth. Above all, the people who work here experience the same concern, respect, and caring attitude they are expected to share externally with every Southwest Customer. By the way, we capitalize the "C" in Customer, and consider that we have two groups of Customers: Internal Customers (employees) and External Customers (the flying public).
>
> We also understand the mission of the airline and its focus on giving people the freedom to fly—without our low fares, they might not otherwise be able to travel. Early on, in the face of continued threats to its existence, Southwest developed a warrior spirit

and a "we can do this" attitude that has evolved into the "whatever it takes" commitment that employees have today.

Rutherford explains that Southwest uses a variety of tools to keep its "Internal Customers" connected and involved with the company's operations.

> We have a department called the University for People that is solely dedicated to employee learning and development— better communication at all levels of the organization is a focal point in all of our leadership training. We also have an Employee Communications and a Legislative Awareness department, both of which are devoted to informing employees about important company issues and legislative issues pertinent to where they live and how those issues might affect them personally or Southwest as a company. These departments use all forms of communication, including a corporate magazine (*Spirit Magazine Luvlines*), a daily electronic bulletin, push e-mail, intranet, extranet, Internet, and a phone hotline to make sure all employees are plugged into what's happening and how and why certain decisions are being made.

Rutherford admits that the company's scrappy reputation has fostered a kind of anything-that-works approach to doing business and solving problems.

As for rules, we have a brief *Guidelines for Leaders* primer that covers legal issues, but as a company we try not to get tied up in procedures that prevent us from doing the right thing for the company or our Customers. Goals are pursued with the mantra: ask forgiveness rather than permission. We try very hard not to get caught up in hierarchies and bureaucratic red tape. We encourage ideas from all strata of the organization and pursue the ones that best match our corporate mission. We also take the time to explain "why not" to the people whose ideas we can't pursue.

When problems come up, we usually create a cross-departmental task force to look at the challenge from all perspectives. This group is charged with finding and implementing solutions and has total support and encouragement from senior management to make its own decisions. We don't subscribe to many formalities, so we forego dry review processes. We find that spontaneous brainstorming is the best way to initiate solutions and then research confirms what will work in our company and what won't.

When asked to name the two or three things that employees would mention if asked to describe what they most appreciate about working at Southwest, Rutherford responded with the following:

Job stability, knowledge of personal role—"I make a difference"—and the intangibles that make each employee feel appreciated and an integral part of a team. They are encouraged to utilize the open-door policy and make known their suggestions and concerns. They know they will get an answer. Healthy workplace relationships are based on mutual respect, which is highly encouraged here. You want to work hard for the success of a team when you respect the people you work with. That respect fosters the community orientation of Southwest Airlines and the easy rapport we have with one another.

Note: In the wake of the September 11, 2001 terrorist attacks and the financial crisis in which airlines—including Southwest—found themselves, Southwest employees offered to work for free until economic conditions improved. The "Pledge to LUV" program (LUV is the company's stock ticker symbol) began in the fourth quarter of 2001 and gave workers the opportunity to "donate" eight hours of free time per pay period. It was an unprecedented gesture but not surprising, given the remarkable devotion of Southwest employees and the fact that the company gave back to its employees a record $180 million in profit sharing in 2000.

Synovus Financial Corp.

Synovus is a regional bank holding company and worldwide financial services provider that was recently named the state of Georgia's top-performing public company. It was also a recent Top-10 pick in *Fortune*'s "100 Best Companies to Work For." To give you an idea of the spirit behind this remarkably successful institution, Bill Turner, whose family started the company more than 100 years ago and who is now chairman of the executive committee, wrote a book called *The Learning of Love: A Journey Toward Servant Leadership.* The book was distributed to each of the company's "family members" with a letter from Turner in the form of a bookmark that began "Synovus: A Culture of the Heart."

Says project manager Michelle Jeffries,

> Our culture is about people. Everything we do we measure against the Golden Rule of treating others, both team members and customers, the way we want to be treated. It's about doing what's right for the individual, celebrating when we enjoy victory and holding hands in times of need. Our strong sense of family goes all the way back to our beginning, when a single act of kindness gave birth to what we now know as Synovus Financial Corp. and our family of companies.
>
> In 1888, G. Gunby Jordan learned that one of the workers at the mill where he served as secretary was almost injured when she caught the hem of her dress in some machinery. The worker was horrified because out of her torn hem had fallen her life savings—she had no safer place, she felt, to keep the

wages she earned. So Mr. Jordan offered to keep her money in the mill's safe and pay her monthly interest—a service he began to offer all the mill workers. He realized that to provide this service properly, he needed to establish a savings bank. That was the beginning of our lead bank, which today we call Columbus Bank and Trust.

Our founders built our company to fulfill the basic need of the people of our first banking community. While we have grown our business to meet the changing needs of our customers, our Culture of the Heart has remained the same. Today, we expect our leaders and all of our team members to Live Our Values, Share Our Vision, and Make Others Successful while Managing the Business. We call these four commitments our Leadership Expectations, and they are at the heart of how we do business every day.

Like other companies committed to supporting honest and ongoing communication between and among employees and departments, the company has an "open-door" policy and uses a variety of print and digital tools (including a magazine—*Connections*—and newsletter) to keep information flowing and missions clear. A good example of Synovus' approach to problem solving is how it responded to an in-house survey finding that "team members" wanted to improve interdepartmental communication. A Communication Action Team quickly came up with a list of recommendations, several of which are presented below:

- Develop "Guidelines for Great Communications"— our expectations for communications accountability.

- Develop training for leaders on how, what, and how often to communicate.

- Encourage visibility of leaders within teams.

- Encourage leaders to observe, coach, and train others on communicating.

- Begin a periodic follow-up survey on communication.

- Better evaluate the appropriate use of both online and print communications.

- Encourage the publication of meeting recaps for team members.

There are also monthly Cultural Trust Meetings led by chairman and CEO Jim Blanchard. "These sessions," says Jeffries, "provide time—often three to four hours—for the chief executive leader of our company to hear from team members."

> Sometimes there's an agenda, but more often the floor is open for whatever people have on their minds. The members of these groups rotate out each year to ensure there is always a fresh perspective. It has become so effective, other senior leaders in each

individual company have begun their own Cultural Trust Committees.

The people who work here continually talk about our culture of caring, the love they have for their coworkers, our generous benefits package, and our support of both their work and life goals and priorities. In fact, it's important to note that we stress to our team members the need to have fun both on and off the job. We encourage departmental and division events and sponsor such things as Team Appreciation Week, barbecue lunches, contests, and so on. We encourage our team leaders to "get away" with their teams occasionally, because we believe having fun together is one of the best ways to build productive lasting relationships and create enthusiasm that is then passed on to our customers.

Texas Nameplate Company

This small manufacturing company sells identification and information labels. It won the Baldrige Award in 1998 and shows up frequently in the literature as a company that is doing things right. TNC uses a variety of listening and learning strategies to identify, anticipate, and then meet the needs of customers, including its "Customer Site Visit" program in which a team of employees goes to a client site to determine how it can improve its products and services. After working with client staff across all departments, the team then reports its findings to *everyone* back at the home office. Independent third-party surveys show that TNC's customers give it consistently high marks in twelve key business areas. Seventy-eight percent of new customers come by way of referral.

And it isn't just customers who are benefiting from the company's people-oriented business philosophy. The results of standardized employee satisfaction surveys are 50 percent higher at TNC than comparative national averages in the five areas that, according to Baldrige Award statistics, are most important to employees: fair pay, job content satisfaction, recognition, fairness/respect, and career development. At TNC's biweekly DO-IT meetings ("daily operations innovation team"), supervisors and team leaders across functional lines come together to problem solve and brainstorm new ideas. TNC has also made significant efforts to address the language challenges of its Spanish-speaking employees, who make up more than 30 percent of the company's workers. It offers a variety of bilingual communication programs as well as tuition reimbursement and paid tutoring for improving language skills.

Tom's of Maine

This family-owned natural personal-care products manufacturer with 135 employees is an eight-time honoree of *Working Mother* magazine's "100 Best Companies," a people-centered and environmentally conscious company that follows the Stewardship Model of doing business: "We believe our company can be profitable and successful while acting in a socially and environmentally responsible manner." The people part of Tom's business success has roots in the company's mission statement, which declares its commitment:

- To build relationships with our customers that extend beyond product usage to include full and honest dialogue, responsiveness to feedback, and the exchange of information about products and issues.

- To respect, value, and serve not only our customers but also our coworkers, owners, agents, suppliers, and our community; to be concerned about and contribute to their well-being; and to operate with integrity so as to be deserving of their trust.

- To provide meaningful work, fair compensation, and a safe, healthy work environment that encourages openness, creativity, self-discipline, and growth.

- To recognize, encourage, and seek a diversity of gifts and perspectives in our worklife.

- To acknowledge the value of each person's contribution to our goals and to foster teamwork in our tasks.

Those five commitments show an abiding appreciation for the role that communication and relationships play in the company's efforts to serve its employees, its customers, and its community. Dialogue, trust, openness, diversity, and teamwork are the very qualities that make up the foundation of a truly successful organization. Importantly, these same qualities seem to go hand-in-hand with a company's financial health. Tom's recently quadrupled its product line in a scant two-year period "without losing sight of our values and mission," a process that is explained in founder Tom Chappell's book *Managing Upside Down: The Seven Intentions of Values-Centered Leadership.* "I have been running our company according to a mission of respecting customers, employees, community, and the environment, and we are creating more products and making more money than I ever dreamed of," he writes in the introduction.

Federal Express

This icon of overnight efficiency and reliability has developed a unique relationship with its employees and customers based on a "people-first" commitment inspired by founder and CEO Frederick Smith. He wanted employees to be an integral part of the decision making process because, as he is quoted on the company website, "When people are placed first they will provide the highest possible service, and profits will follow." From this principle came the FedEx corporate philosophy—People-Service-Profit—which forms the basis for all business decisions:

- The people priority acknowledges the importance of employee satisfaction and empowerment to create an environment where employees feel secure enough to take risks and become innovative in pursuing quality, service, and customer satisfaction.

- Service refers to the consistent and clearly stated service quality goal of 100 percent customer satisfaction, 100 percent of the time.

- A corporate profit should result if the people and service goals have been met.

- Within that philosophy are a number of specific programs, each impressive in its scope and purpose:

Survey Feedback Action (SFA)

This annual employee survey provides a statistical measurement of employee satisfaction, as well as staff opinions of management's leadership performance. Each April, every employee is asked to participate in an online survey that asks thirty-two questions relating to the company in general and to the employee's superiors. Managers then hold feedback sessions with their employees to discuss the survey findings and identify problems within and outside their department. As a group, they develop formal, written action plans for solving these problems. Groups usually review plans throughout the year to determine whether problems were solved satisfactorily.

Open Door

This program encourages employees to question or file a complaint about matters of corporate policy such as benefits, hiring, seniority, vacation, and so on. An actual Open Door form is used, which is then routed by Employee Relations to the management person best able to respond to the issue. The person receiving the Open Door inquiry must respond within fourteen calendar days.

Guaranteed Fair Treatment Procedure (GFTP)

This program ensures that every employee complaint or grievance is heard; it is, essentially, an employee appeals process. It is designed to deal with employees' more personal issues, as opposed to the general policy issues addressed by Open Door. These could include disputed performance reviews, disciplinary actions, termination, and job postings that employees feel they should have been seriously considered for yet weren't. Employees must first try to resolve their grievance with their manager or supervisor before pursuing the GFTP.

Sounds True

This homegrown company of sixty employees in Boulder, Colorado, specializes in producing and distributing spirituality, personal growth, and alternative medicine music and spoken-word audiotapes and CDs. In the same way that Sounds True seeks to educate its customers with such consciousness-expanding products, it strives to bring a similar commitment to how it runs its business. This includes a fifteen-minute "contemplative time-out" every morning at

11:00, Monday-morning business sessions between management and staff, ongoing peer-to-peer review processes, and an emphasis on collaborative decision making. The company is also well aware that bills need to be paid, so it recently started an open-book management program to educate all its employees on the financial realities and challenges of running Sounds True.

Not surprisingly, the company's mission is driven by strong values, and of the twenty that make up the list, quite a few address the importance of honest communication and healthy interpersonal relations. These include:

- We build workplace community.

- We encourage authenticity.

- We encourage open communication.

- Teams determine the best way to reach their goals.

- We have a relationship with our customers that is based on integrity.

- We take time for kindness, have fun, and get a lot done.

- We acknowledge that every person in the organization carries wisdom.

- We encourage people to speak up and propose solutions.

- We encourage people to listen deeply.

- We honor individual differences and diversity.
- We strive for clarity of expectations.

Business Without Walls

The quality of communication that people have with one another in any given company cannot be separated from how those employees are treated and what the company values as the key to its success. All the businesses profiled here have specific programs and policies designed to keep doors open and information flowing and to give their employees every opportunity to help shape the company's present and future. There is a high level of trust in such an environment; with so few restrictions and so much interaction, little is hidden from staff or management. And yet that is the secret to the vitality these companies exhibit, measured by the enthusiasm of the people who work there and the depth of their loyalties. A company has no greater value than the collective wisdom of its employees. Give them a chance to express that wisdom, and there is little that a company won't accomplish.

CHAPTER 9

"I long to accomplish a great and noble task, but it is my chief duty to accomplish humble tasks as though they were great and noble. The world is moved along, not only by the mighty shoves of its heroes, but also by the aggregate of tiny pushes of each honest worker."

—HELEN KELLER

"Two roads diverged in a wood, and I—I took the one less traveled, and that has made all the difference."

—ROBERT FROST

Who Do You Want to Be?

People communicate all the time, at many levels, in many situations, and for many purposes. Sometimes this communication consists of nothing more than a hello when we walk through the office door in the morning; other times is goes to the heart of a company's mission, how it envisions its role in the lives of its employees and in the community it serves. Much of the emphasis in this book has been on the deceptive complexity that underlies what we say, how we say it, and why we say it.

In chapter 1 I talked about the influence of a company's culture on the willingness and even the ability of people to talk openly and honestly with one another about important issues that affect their work. Chapter 2 took an honest look at why so many people are angry at their jobs, how difficult it is to speak up about it, and some of the ways to attend to those feelings. Chapter 3 discussed the role of gender at work and how women and men approach their jobs and each other differently. Chapters 4, 5, and 6 focused on the relationship dynamics among coworkers, between managers and staff, and between a company and the customers who support it. Working in groups was the subject of chapter 7, and chapter 8 celebrated a handful of companies that have built successful businesses by putting people and relationships ahead of everything else—all of which brings us to here.

It can seem a daunting task trying to make sense of it all, learning when to say what to whom and how, while juggling all the concerns and feelings that fill our workaday lives. Constant deadlines, incompetent bosses, unfair policies, planetary misalignments—these and a thousand other things beyond our control make it difficult to be our best. The pressures to go along, to play the game, to succumb to the status quo conspire to keep us from breaking through. And yet break through we must, step by careful step, to transform our workplace into the kind of environment where people feel counted and a sense of community is more than a corporate slogan.

As we try to figure out how the pieces fit together, how to make the best of each situation we encounter, it may help to ask—and keep asking—ourselves the following two questions: Who do I want to be at work? What kind of impact do I want to make?

The first question speaks to whatever ambitions we have to improve ourselves as human beings—think New Year's Eve resolutions, but go a little deeper. Every day at work we make choices: how much effort to put out, what information to share or to withhold, how open we'll be to another point of view, and so on. The sum total of these choices is who we are as "workers." This book has presented many such choices, each one directed at transforming the way we communicate and build relationships with our coworkers. They are choices of intention and technique and attitude and behavior. The difference between the choices we're making now and the ones suggested in this book is one measure of who we are at work and who we can become.

The second question is related to the first. It acknowledges that we can make a difference and then challenges us to do so consciously. It doesn't mean that we need always to assess our situation in a strategic way, plotting how A leads to B and then hopefully to C or D. It means that our actions count, that what we do affects the people around us and, in the end, the success or failure of the company that employs us. Being more aware of those causes-and-effects (however modest they may be) *and intending them to be positive and life-affirming* is one of the key conditions under which communication miracles can occur.

Reaching for Something Greater

At one level, achieving better communication and stronger relationships at work is simply a matter of developing better people skills. Treating your colleagues with dignity and respect, listening when they talk, and letting them know that you understand what they need are examples of specific actions that can put others at ease so they don't feel wary or aggressive. By "disarming" others in this way, you're more

> We're talking about our jobs becoming a place where we continue to grow as human beings and, in turn, to grow the organization along with us.

likely to make your own needs and ideas clear, work gets done quicker and less painfully, and you've improved the likelihood that future relations will be just as productive. The best salespeople do this all the time, motivated by the desire to make a sale but also well aware that unless they treat potential customers with a certain degree of genuine respect, chances of gaining their trust will be low.

At another level we're talking about our jobs becoming a place where we continue to grow as human beings and, in turn, to grow the organization along with us. Change happens when we take a risk. How much more powerful to let your coworker know immediately if something she did troubled you and why than to keep it bottled up. While she may not respond in a way you'd like her to, the payoff is that you stepped outside your comfort zone and pushed the boundaries of your experience into a new area. You will have learned something about your own strengths and given that other person a chance to learn something about hers. "The freedom to express your real feelings," write William and Kathleen Lundin in *The Healing Manager,* "is the beginning of creativity."

I believe that resistance to new ways of working together

is getting weaker as the need for authenticity grows stronger. "I'm so tired of all the games," said one frustrated woman. "I just want people at work to tell it like it is and treat me like an intelligent human being."

More and more people are yearning for meaningful contact, for something beyond functional necessity. We want to be understood, to do what we think is right, to feel good about ourselves and about others. We're looking around for answers, and in the daily give-and-take of our workplace routines we will begin to find them as we each take our own first steps forward. These won't necessarily lead to miracles of the blinding white light variety but to something much more human, imbedded gems in the gritty realities of working with those around us.

So whether your goals are modest or far-reaching, whether you just want to get along better with the guy or gal in the next cubicle or you want nothing less than a department-wide communication transformation, here are a final few reminders to help keep you focused and grounded.

• *Start from zero.* Your perspective of a situation is not necessarily the largest or truest. Everyone involved in a problem or a disagreement or an exchange of views has a piece of the truth to contribute. Good communication is as much about learning as it is about sharing. Our responsibility as communication maestros is to embrace all interactions as a process of self-discovery and truth seeking, a place to observe, ask questions, and not assume. "Beginner's mind" is a wonderful place from which to discover the deeper patterns of workplace entanglements and opportunities.

• *Know thyself.* It's true that a company's leadership and its policies have an enormous effect on the atmosphere of honesty where you work and that situations and people will come at you from a lot of directions over which you have little or no control. But as important as it is to understand the culture where you work and how it affects the way you communicate, it's even more essential to be in touch with the inner culture of your own personality. How you interpret the actions of others, what your particular needs and biases are, and so on, either enhance your communication skills or diminish them. Being honest about your weaknesses, facing up to your denials, addictions, fears, and resentments, will help you realize when you are part of the problem. As you start to recognize the impact of these issues—authority problems with a boss, jealousy of a coworker—on the people and the situations where you work, they'll lose their power, and you'll begin making different, and healthier, decisions.

• *All for one, and one for all.* You are part of a community that includes the people with whom you work and the people you serve. As you become more sensitized to yourself, practice extending that sensitivity to others. This practice will heighten your awareness of what is needed in any given situation. It doesn't mean that you ignore your own needs, but it does ask you to expand your idea of self-interest to include all the relationships that are part of where you work.

You certainly can't control what goes on in the rest of the company, but when you start to see what you do as connected to the larger whole, your attitude and behavior take on a different meaning. You aren't marching alone but in concert with everyone else, and the importance of relationship grows.

When Joyce Fletcher wrote about "relational theory" in her book *Disappearing Acts* (excerpted in chapter 2), she described it as a model of group behavior where "growth-fostering interactions are characterized by mutual empathy and mutual empowerment, where both parties recognize vulnerability as part of the human condition, approach the interaction expecting to grow from it, and feel a responsibility to contribute to the growth of the other." She is focusing here on a more personal level, but the image can be extended to include an entire company. The best workplaces aren't "us versus them" but "we."

• *Don't be afraid of intimacy.* The word *intimacy* is not necessarily about emotional and physical closeness, which is what we usually think of when we hear the word. It actually comes from the Latin *intimatus,* meaning to make something known to someone else. In the context of work, this concept speaks directly to the way we communicate. In the context of this book, it asks us to be willing to step out of our various roles and to deal with one another as people and not as positions. Yes, legitimate authority issues exist, but they shouldn't prevent us from an honest sharing of thoughts, ideas, and concerns, one person to another. Whether among coworkers or between managers and staff or staff and customers, communication in the spirit of intimacy says that we recognize one another's common humanity and aren't afraid to step closer to who they are. This also means that we drop our guard to let someone else in. It takes practice and the buildup of trust, but a truly intimate workplace will ultimately feed far more than just our pocketbook.

• *Embrace conflict*... but always seek resolution. Conflict and disagreement offer wonderful opportunities to learn and grow. As long as you respect others' differences and things don't get personal, as long as you question the idea and not the person, then there will be room for discovery and movement toward a best solution. Disagreements over methods based on objective information is a much cleaner path to problem solving than "my way versus your way" tug-of-wars. Don't let your ego get in the way of "seeking the highest good."

• *Do it anyway.* Not everyone will respond the way you want them to when you start becoming more honest and trusting and other-centered at work. Some people may actually feel threatened because you aren't playing by the old rules anymore. They may see weakness instead of strength and turn it into some kind of an advantage. You may have wonderful ideas for transforming your department, but if your boss or your boss' boss won't give you the support you need, it will be a struggle Not all will go smoothly when you buck the status quo. But the point of committing to breakthrough communication is to do it without guarantees of a fair return. Why? Because it's the right thing to do. And sometimes all it takes is one brave act to start a revolution.

• *It makes dollar sense.* There is little question that an open and trusting environment valuing honest communication and respectful workplace relationships leads to healthy bottom lines. When employees' needs are taken seriously and their aspirations supported, when they believe that a company cares about who they are, then they will happily give themselves to the corporate cause. Most people want to be a productive part of a successful organization; any investment made in their essential goodness will pay back many times over.

Some Final Thoughts

So much has been written about the sorry state of our workplaces, and it's true that years of abuse and neglect have led to fearful, cynical environments where communication is used more often as a weapon than a tool. This book has not shied away from acknowledging those problems. But it's equally clear that for companies to meet the challenges of the twenty-first century, they will have to cultivate an atmosphere of trust and learning where people treat one another with compassion, caring, and respect. That, too, is a message that has resonated throughout these pages. We are facing some difficult choices about how to create a future that works—personally, economically, culturally, and collectively. What values will guide us? Who do we want to be?

The tips in this book may help bring a little more peace to your working life. They may even nudge corporate decision-makers to rethink their approach to employee and customer relations. What I really hope to have accomplished is to show what the workplace could feel like if a true spirit of community was present, created by a committed group of people who value each other as they work toward achieving a common vision. As the walls between us come down and our true humanity emerges, as we start "talking our walk," that potential will surely become a reality.

Resources

Books

Arnott, Dave. *Corporate Cults: The Insidious Lure of the All-Consuming Organization.* New York: Amacom, 1999.

Barlow, Janelle, and Claus Møller. *A Complaint Is a Gift: Using Customer Feedback as a Strategic Tool.* San Francisco: Berrett-Kohler, 1996.

Bassman, Emily S. *Abuse in the Workplace: Management Remedies and Bottom Line Impact.* Westport, CT: Greenwood Publishing Group, 1992.

Bell, Chip R. *Customers as Partners: Building Relationships That Last.* San Francisco: Berrett-Kohler, 1994.

Bohm, David. *On Dialogue.* New York: Routledge, 1996.

Bollier, David. *Aiming Higher: 25 Stories of How Companies Prosper By Combining Sound Management and Social Vision.* New York: Amacom, 1996.

Campbell, Susan. *From Chaos to Confidence: Survival Strategies for the New Workplace.* New York: Simon & Schuster, 1995.

Chambers, Harry E. *Effective Communication Skills: For Scientific and Technical Professionals.* Cambridge: Perseus Publishing, 2001.

Chappell, Tom. *Managing Upside Down: The Seven Intentions of Values-Centered Leadership.* New York: Avon, 1999.

Childre, Doc, and Bruce Cryer. *Freeze-Frame®—One-Minute Stress Management: A Scientifically Proven Technique for Clear Decision Making and Improved Health.* Boulder Creek, CA: Planetary Publications, 1998.

Cooper, Cary L., and Steve Williams. *Creating Healthy Organizations.* New York: Wiley, 1994.

Fletcher, Joyce. *Disappearing Acts: Gender, Power, and Relational Practice at Work.* Cambridge: MIT Press, 1999.

Gatto, Rex. *Controlling Stress in the Workplace: Turning Stress into Productivity.* San Francisco: Pfeiffer, 1993.

Goldsmith, Joan, and Kenneth Cloke. *Thank God It's Monday: 14 Values We Need to Humanize the Way We Work.* New York: McGraw-Hill, 1996.

Goleman, Daniel, and Cary Cherniss. *The Emotionally Intelligent Workplace: How to Select for, Measure, and Improve Emotional Intelligence in Individuals, Groups, and Organizations.* San Francisco: Jossey-Bass, 2001.

Kanter, Rosabeth Moss. *Men and Women of the Corporation.* New York: Basic Books, 1977.

Kottler, Jeffrey A. *Beyond Blame: A New Way of Resolving Conflicts in Relationships.* San Francisco: Jossey-Bass, 1994.

Lundin, William and Kathleen. *The Healing Manager: How to Build Quality Relationships and Productive Cultures at Work.* San Francisco: Berrett-Kohler, 1993.

Morgan, Rebecca L. *Calming Upset Customers: Staying Effective During Unpleasant Situations.* Menlo Park, CA: Crisp Publications, 1996.

Reardon, Kathleen Kelley. *They Don't Get It, Do They? Communication in the Workplace—Closing the Gap Between Women and Men.* New York: Little, Brown, 1996.

Reichheld, Frederick F., et al. *The Loyalty Effect: The Hidden Force Behind Growth, Profits, and Lasting Change.* New York: McGraw-Hill, 1996.

Reina, Michelle L. and Dennis S. *Trust and Betrayal in the Workplace: Building Effective Relationships in Your Organization.* San Francisco: Berrett-Kohler, 1999.

Rosenbluth, Hal F., and Diane McFerrin Peters. *Care to Compete? Secrets from America's Best Companies on Managing with People and Profits in Mind.* Cambridge: Perseus Books, 1999.

Ryan, Kathleen D., and Daniel K. Oestreich. *Driving Fear Out of the Workplace: How to Overcome the Invisible Barriers to Quality, Productivity, and Innovation.* San Francisco: Jossey-Bass, 1991.

Schwarz, Roger M. *The Skilled Facilitator: Practical Wisdom for Developing Effective Groups.* San Francisco: Jossey-Bass, 1994.

Senge, Peter, et al. *The Fifth Discipline Fieldbook: Strategies and Tools for Building a Learning Organization.* New York: Doubleday, 1994.

Short, Ronald R. *Learning in Relationship: Foundation for Personal and Professional Success.* Seattle: Learning in Action Technologies, 1998.

Tannen, Deborah. *Talking from 9 to 5: Women and Men in the Workplace—Language, Sex and Power.* New York: Avon, 1994.
_____. *You Just Don't Understand: Women and Men in Conversation.* New York: Avon, 1990.

Terez, Tom. *22 Keys to Creating a Meaningful Workplace.* Avon, MA: Adams Media, 2000.

Wilmot, William, and Elaine Yarbrough. *Artful Mediation: Constructive Conflict at Work.* Boulder: Cairns Publishing, 1995.

Wilson, Paul. *Calm at Work: Breeze Through Your Day Feeling Calm, Relaxed and in Control.* New York: Plume, 1999.

Websites

Advancing Women
www.advancingwomen.com

This award-winning, resource-rich website provides coaching, mentoring, strategy, and support services for working women, with a particular emphasis on the role of technology and how it can be used to advance one's career.

Bully OnLine
www.successunlimited.co.uk/bully

This U.K. website, the brainchild of Tim Field, founder of the U.K. National Workplace Bullying Advice Line, really is "the world's leading resource on bullying and related issues." The many articles are quite long and the site is densely organized, but there is nothing like it on the Web for those looking for in-depth insight on the phenomenon of bullying.

BusinessEthics
www.business-ethics.com

This website specializes in monitoring "corporate social responsibility" and is loaded with research, articles, and networking resources, as well as excerpts and archives from the award-winning *Business Ethics* magazine. BE also sponsors The 100 Best Corporate Citizens annual awards.

Center for Nonviolent Communication
www.cnvc.org

This website is built around Marshall Rosenberg's approach to resolving personal and professional conflict, presented in his book *Nonviolent Communication: A Language of Compassion.* It acts as both a training site for practitioners of NVC (nonviolent communication) and an informational site for laypeople.

Consortium for Research on Emotional Intelligence in Organizations
www.eiconsortium.org

Founded in the spring of 1996 with the support of the Fetzer Institute, the Consortium's mission is to aid the advancement of research and practice related to "emotional intelligence" in workplaces and organizations. To that end the site features plenty of downloadable reports and training programs, reference materials, links, and so on.

Customer Care Institute
www.customercare.com

This organization and its resource-rich website provide research, advisory services, and training and networking opportunities for "customer-care" professionals, including studies, white papers, booklets, newsletters, forums, workshops, and conferences.

eComplaints.com
www.ecomplaints.com

By giving consumers a place to vent their frustrations and companies a chance to respond, this unique website has created a forum for sellers and buyers to work through issues often brought about through poor communication. Includes a Top 10 list of most "e-complained-about" companies.

Employer-Employee.com
www.employer-employee.com

This is a true portal site for workers of all stripes, with many layers of work-enhancing and problem-solving tips, products, resources, links, and articles, equally dedicated to the needs of managers, the managed, and the intersection of the two.

The Facilitator
www.TheFacilitator.com

This is the website version of the quarterly newsletter of the same name, featuring archived articles, book reviews, tips, techniques, and more, including an extensive links section to other resources and user groups around the country.

Hard@Work
www.hardatwork.com

The mission of this hip, lively website is "to reduce the oversupply of fear and alienation in the workplace by meeting the pent-up demand for constructive communication about what's happening on the job." It features discussion groups at The Water Cooler, advice from The Mentor, case studies in The Rock Pile, an informative free newsletter, and other useful tools for addressing real-world issues at work.

Intercultural Communication Institute
www.intercultural.org

This private, nonprofit foundation is dedicated to building awareness of and appreciation for cultural differences in our communities and in our workplaces by offering consulting services and training intercultural practitioners. Its new website introduces visitors to founder Dr. Milton Bennett's approach to diversity management and the Institute's growing educational offerings.

Life in the USA
www.lifeintheusa.com

This site is dedicated to helping newcomers to the United States understand the culture and values of American society. Straightforward articles by site founder Elliot Essman cover such topics as religion, finance, the workplace, citizenship, health care, and more, including relevant links. It is an informational site only; Essman explicitly resists giving immigration advice.

MeaningfulWorkplace.com
www.meaningfulworkplace.com

This is the popular website of author and speaker Tom Terez. It focuses largely on the results of his extensive workplace survey that identified twenty-two "keys" to a healthy workplace (see book reference above), but other features have been added, most recently an Awesome and Awful Boss Hall of Fame and a Showcase of Winning Workplaces.

The Message Company/Business Spirit Journal Online
www.bizspirit.com

The Message Company itself sponsors workshops on consciousness and business, while the journal offers information, inspiration, and resources for those wanting to broaden the definition of "bottom line" to include spirit, heart, personal satisfaction, and global sustainability.

MSN
www.msn.com

This major online portal has a few interactive message boards devoted to workplace issues, including Disgruntled Workers and Office Talk. Like other such boards on the web they draw their share of sales pitches and inappropriate posters, but they can also be a place for people to safely download their frustrations and find helpful input and support.

The Ombudsman Association
www.ombuds-toa.org

The Ombudsman Association (TOA) is a nonprofit, international organization dedicated to serving the needs and practice of professional ombudspeople. The primary job of these "designated neutrals" is to address organizational disputes and enhance organizational communication.

Society for Human Resource Management
www.shrm.org

SHRM provides education and information services, conferences and seminars, government and media representation, and online services and publications to more than 165,000 professional and student members throughout the world. It is the world's largest human resource management association.

Workforce
www.workforce.com

This excellent website builds on the success of the same-named monthly magazine, with plenty of insightful tools and interactive forums for human resource professionals.

Working Wounded
www.workingwounded.com

Working Wounded was founded by syndicated newspaper columnist Bob Rosner, author of *The Boss's Survival Guide* (McGraw-Hill, 2001) and *Working Wounded: Advice that Adds Insight to Injury* (Warner Books, 1998). This irreverent but informative site is highly interactive, featuring interviews, "confessionals," messages, photos, links, and more.

Personality in the Workplace

What do *you* bring to the workplace? The following books and websites will help you explore your "inner culture," the temperament, behavior, and attitudes that make up who you are and influence how you act at work. They aren't infallible sources, but are good places to begin a process of self-discovery.

Dempcy, Mary H., and Rene Tihista. *Dear Job Stressed: Answers for the Overworked, Overwrought, and Overwhelmed.* Palo Alto, CA: Davies-Black, 1996.

Elston, Lee. *Square Pegs and Round Holes: How to Match Personality to the Job.* San Diego: First Step Enterprises, 1984.

Hoffman, Edward. *Ace the Corporate Personality Test.* New York: McGraw-Hill, 2001.

Janda, Louis. *Career Tests: 25 Revealing Self-Tests to Help You Find and Succeed at the Perfect Career.* Avon, MA: Adams Media, 1999.

Keirsey, David, and Marilyn Bates. *Please Understand Me: Character and Temperament Types.* Amherst, NY: Prometheus Books, 1984.

Myers, Isabel Briggs and Peter B. *Gifts Differing.* Palo Alto, CA: Consulting Psychologists Press, 1990.

Palmer, Helen. *The Enneagram Advantage: Putting the 9 Personality Types to Work at the Office.* New York: Three Rivers Press, 1998.

DiscoverME
www.discoverme.com
This corporate personality-matching website offers online testing

and assessment technology services to both employers and would-be employees.

The Enneagram
www.authenticenneagram.com
www.9types.com
www.enneagram.net

These are three of many sites dedicated to the study of the Enneagram. They each feature introductory and historical information, chat rooms or message boards, and descriptions of the nine primary personality types. AuthenticEnneagram is the most sophisticated of the three, while 9types focuses more heavily on the types themselves and includes an easy self-test for determining your own type.

LifeExplore.com
www.geocities.com/lifexplore

Although this site hadn't been updated since August 2000, it still offers an excellent introduction to the field of personality psychology, including its roots in the work of Carl Jung and descriptions of some of the methodologies that followed. There is a Resource and Community center and links to more than fifty tests.

TypeLogic
www.typelogic.com

A good site if you want to know more about the Meyers-Briggs typing system and its sixteen primary personality types.

Acknowledgments

I would like to start by thanking the capable and committed staff at Conari, especially my editor, Leslie Berriman, whose keen eye and gracious manner were indispensable to the making of this book. Special thanks to BJ Gallagher, who took time out from a very busy schedule to write an affirmative an enthusiastic foreword. I also owe gratitude to Kathy and Holly of the Orcas Island Public Library, who allowed me to exceed my interlibrary loan limits and thus overcome my island-bound isolation. The staff at the Rock Creek campus library of Portland Community College was also generous in giving this nonstudent access to their computers at a critical time in the writing and research process.

My wife, Nancy, was, as always, a constant source of support and insight. I'm indebted to Mary Ann Owen, an organizational consultant who offered many insights from her years on the corporate front lines. Thanks also to the folks at TDIndustries, SAS Institute, Southwest Airlines, and Synovus Corp. for taking the time to answer my questions about their work culture and their approach to communication. This book also stands on the shoulders of those whose works are listed in Resources. Their collaborative efforts on behalf of workplace transformation have inspired a great many. To those who agreed to review the manuscript and found merit enough to endorse it, your words of support meant a lot. And, finally, I'd like to thank everyone else who contributed to this book (some of whose names have been changed), by sharing their stories of workplace frustration and, in a few cases, of triumph. Your experiences speak for many and gave this book the grounding it needed to show that while communication challenges are very real, the tools to overcome them are ever present.

Index

About the Author

MATTHEW GILBERT is a writer, editor, facilitator, and communication consultant who has served in a variety of management positions over the past twenty years. For seven of those years he was the managing editor of *NAPRA ReView,* the country's leading lifestyle trade magazine in the body/mind/spirit marketplace. He is the author of the book *Take This Job and Love It: How to Find Fulfillment in Any Job You Do,* and numerous articles on health, psychology, and personal growth. Matthew lives with his wife Nancy on a houseboat near Portland, Oregon.

For more information on Matthew Gilbert
and topics covered in his book, see
www.communicationmiraclesatwork.com

To Our Readers

Conari Press publishes books on topics ranging from spirituality, personal growth, and relationships to women's issues, parenting, and social issues. Our mission is to publish quality books that will make a difference in people's lives-how we feel about ourselves and how we relate to one another. We value integrity, compassion, and receptivity, both in the books we publish and in the way we do business.

As a member of the community, we donate our damaged books to nonprofit organizations, dedicate a portion of our proceeds from certain books to charitable causes, and continually look for new ways to use natural resources as wisely as possible.

Our readers are our most important resource, and we value your input, suggestions, and ideas about what you would like to see published. Please feel free to contact us, to request our latest book catalog, or to be added to our mailing list.

2550 Ninth Street, Suite 101
Berkeley, California 94710-2551
800-685-9595 • 510-649-7175
fax: 510-649-7190 • e-mail: conari@conari.com
www.conari.com